S0-AEG-740

Labour in
American politics

Labour in
American politics

Vivian Vale

Lecturer in Politics
University of Southampton

New York
Barnes & Noble, Inc.

First published in Great Britain 1971
Published in The United States of America 1971
by Barnes & Noble, Inc., New York, N.Y. 10003
© *Vivian Vale, 1971*
ISBN 389 04088 6

Printed in Great Britain

Contents

To
Jim Larson
Carolinian host

1

Labour and the American environment

The realm of Anglo-American studies does not appear on every map of Academe. But wherever its territorial boundaries are demarcated, we may be sure that they incorporate the province of labour. As an area of study, that province owes its cohesiveness to an affinity between its British and American departments which neither time nor space has obliterated. It was apparent when the British immigrant brought over his skills, both technical and organizational, to the journeymen of the young republic's eastern towns. It is in evidence today when British and American labour federations exchange fraternal delegates (as they have done uninterruptedly since 1894), or send representatives to collaborate side by side in the International Confederation of Free Trade Unions.

Throughout the intervening continuum of labour history, this Anglo-American affinity manifests itself in various forms. American law, for instance, as applied to burgeoning trade unions was developed largely out of English common law. In both countries, government's attitude towards unionism evolved historically through the same successive phases: from suppression to toleration to benevolence to regulation. Union organization itself followed somewhat similar stages of development on both sides of the Atlantic, though often with a time lag of about a generation. The early objective of 'general unionism of all the productive classes', typified by Robert Owen's Grand National

Consolidated, has had its American counterparts in the National Labour Union and the Knights of Labour. The contraction of British unionism in the second half of the nineteenth century to a base narrowly protective of the skilled crafts is paralleled by the restrictive and exclusive policies of the American Federation of Labour (AFL) from the 1880s onward. If the Federation's leaders were cool towards political engagement, so were the Junta's. The AFL's national conventions rebuffed the Socialists as firmly as did Broadhurst and his colleagues at their Dundee conference of 1889. And if many American unionists and their officers have participated individually in politics as unashamed Republicans, one may recall that as late as 1906 British unionists were standing for parliament as Conservative party candidates. Many distinguished American labour leaders were British-born, from Richard Trevellick to Philip Murray, and including the first president of the AFL, Samuel Gompers. It was hearing Thomas Hughes and A. J. Mundella speak in New York in 1870 that first gave Gompers seriously to ponder the true character and functions of the trade union. From English unions he copied the device of equalization of funds, whereby the more prosperous branches ('locals') could fortify the weaker. The AFL's jurisdictional (*Anglice*, 'demarcation') rules had much in common with those formalized by the TUC at Bridlington.

The affinity extends to our own century. If in the first two or three decades the craft leaders of the AFL looked askance on the growing mass of industrial workers, this was how their British congeners had regarded the new unionism of Tillett, Mann and Thorne. If Gompers and his colleagues declined to adapt the AFL's organizational patterns to embrace the new unskilled, we may remind ourselves that both unionists like George Howell and intellectuals like the Webbs doubted whether the existing conformation of unions 'coextensive with craft', as in the NUR, could be bettered. Again, as short-lived twentieth-century essays in high-level collaboration between unionism and business in the ostensible interest of public economic good, the National Civic Federation, operative for a few years in the USA, may bear some comparison with the Mond-Turner experiment here. The Taft-Hartley Act came to American unions in 1947 with as great a shock as the Trades

Disputes and Trade Unions Act had come to the British twenty years before. And if the American labour-management field has been subject to greater legislative control than our own, present British discontents with industrial relations suggest that this may not continue indefinitely the case.

Yet a point-by-point comparison of labour's political activity in the respective countries may leave the observer convinced that these resemblances are not of the essence, and that it is the differences that run deeper. In contrast with their British confrères, American workers have displayed a very low degree of class-consciousness. America's trade unionism, unlike its business, was comparatively late in converting its potential influence into stable political pressures. Right up until the New Deal it relied primarily upon piecemeal economic methods of self-advancement, and in bad times its attention was readily diverted to other expedients than labour parties. While the British trade unions in the early 1870s were setting up their Labour Representation League and returning their first members to parliament, American labour associations were dividing over the merits of Greenbackism. While the British movement in the 1890s was feeling its way towards a party of its own, the most promising transatlantic labour body, the AFL, had turned its back upon corporate political engagement. By the time the latter was preparing to bring its first cautious pressures to bear upon Washington, in 1906, fifty-two Labour MPs were being sent to Westminster. In the following year, while they were helping the Trades Disputes Act on to the statute book, a major American union was being paralysed by the most comprehensive labour injunction a court had ever imposed. The early New Deal tried unsuccessfully to achieve by voluntary methods the drawing-up for each industry of labour codes of the kind that the British parliament had been promulgating since 1890. The election manifesto of 1945 *Let Us Face the Future* proclaimed that 'the Labour Party is a socialist party and proud of it'; and that election itself gave Labour nearly four hundred seats. At the same juncture American labour was facing the spectre of post-war mass unemployment and severe legislative assault on its collective bargaining freedoms, while one wing at least of its socialist movement lay under statutory proscription. As for the influence of gradual and ameliorative socialism, although the first Fabian tract was indeed written by an American, union leaders in the USA have tended to dismiss experts of the Webbian stripe as 'the professors' or 'the social worker crowd'.

Sketchy as such comparisons may be, they appear to demonstrate that, while Anglo-American resemblances have recurred most frequently in the economic sphere, the divergences are predominantly in the political. Over there, it seems, labour is less concerned with politics and less involved with government. At first sight this impression may strike the casual British reader of the transatlantic press as unconvincing. He will note that the programme submitted by the biggest American labour federation to the platform committees of the major parties in 1968 began with half-a-dozen planks on foreign policy. Its biennial convention reports contain resolutions, carried unanimously, calling for Congressional action on international affairs, consumer protection, civil rights, legislative reapportionment, lowering of the voting age, abolition of the Electoral College, an end to Senatorial filibusters and fuller representation for the District of Columbia. What could be more political than that? 'We have reached the time', said America's most senior union official nearly twenty years ago, 'when it is beyond question that politics is imperatively number one trade union business, and when the ballot has become our most important weapon in the struggle for survival.'

Closer study of the movement nevertheless confirms the impression of a deep-seated difference in American labour's attitude to politics. Some engagement there has always been, ever since the artisans of early nineteenth-century Philadelphia formed their clubs to promote 'the general diffusion of constitutional, legal and political knowledge among the working people'. Yet preoccupation with politics was for the next hundred years intermittent not stable, isolated not general, limited not comprehensive in aim, the palliative of depression not the instrument of social change. Even after the New Deal made government an efficient instrument of social and economic reform, labour has preferred a pressure-group to a party role. Thereby it has repeatedly disappointed those British labourites who, whether practical men like Robert Smillie or theoreticians like Harold Laski, have believed that American unionism could mature only by developing a party of its own.

How shall we account for this political abstemiousness? One kind of explanation may be looked for in the strictly limited, though intensely fought over, ground of economic contention between labour and capital in the United States. 'Regardless,' said one president of the AFL shortly after World War II, 'of how capital and labour may disagree upon other economic, social and political questions, they stand united in defence of the maintenance of our free enterprise system and of the joint benefits which derive therefrom.' 'We like the system under which we live,' echoed his successor ten years later, 'we merely say that we as workers want a fair share of the wealth.' Certainly in no other country of the world have workers so fully adapted themselves to the economic system they have found. Throughout most of its one hundred and fifty years of life, organized labour (a phrase first used by an American President in a message of Theodore Roosevelt to Congress) has concurred with the premises of American capitalism, has propagated the gospel of wealth and the myth of rugged individualism, and has shared the American dream. Its unions have been at least as much concerned with the creation of wealth as with its distribution: the *American Federationist*, journal of the AFL, has carried full-page advertisements of business corporations urging its readership to purchase stocks and shares. Beatrice Webb noted in her diary how one AFL delegate to the TUC congress of 1926 'was appointed *while present at the Congress* to a post of £5,000 a year in a capitalistic undertaking and did not trouble to stay out the first two days'. For Gompers, the AFL's president, it was a high desideratum that labour should achieve an acceptability, legitimacy and esteem in American society on a par with business or the Church.

Today American labour leaders administer insurance companies and speculate in real estate. One recent leader of the Teamsters' union, Dave Beck, whose huge property transactions attracted the unfavourable attention of Congress and the courts, was a leading Elk, a regent of the University of Washington, a man who professed to abhor strikes and who opposed the public ownership of electric power, who maintained his private stud, trainers and jockeys, and negotiated with employers at the country club level. The very large salaries, allowances and perquisites enjoyed by the modern union boss are alleged to give a vicarious satisfaction to his followers, who see him bargaining with management on the same social footing.

European observers have therefore been struck by a paradox. If unions and management shared the same economic creed, why the bitter conflict, reaching pinnacles of armed violence in the railroad riots of 1877, the Homestead steel and Pullman company strikes of 1892 and 1894, involving pitched battles, the sending in of federal troops and a Presidential commission of inquiry? Why the prolonged and bloody troubles in the West Virginian coalfields from 1911 to 1919, the turbulence in mass-production industries of the mid-1930s? American labour-management quarrels (so the explanation would seem to run) have been all the more acrimonious for being about the dividing of the identically same spoils – the product of the system both sides basically accept. Businesses and unions wear the appearance of competing power systems, monopoly and counter-monopoly, locked in deadly antagonism over the means of holding or winning a respectively larger share of the fruits of industry. Collective bargaining American-style is no frontal assault on property rights, but the collision of two conceptions of property where the possessiveness of the employer towards the conduct of his business encounters the possessiveness of the employee towards the conditions of his job.

So narrowly indeed was the contest confined within the economic arena, with so little reliance placed by labour on the state as more than ring-keeper, that – paradoxically – when government at last entered the field it had to do much that in Britain could be left to industry and labour jointly. The New Deal Administration within the space of three years had to provide statutory guarantees of the workers' freedom to organize, an entire framework of collective bargaining, and machinery to settle inter-union disputes. In the Second World War, when in Britain wage control could be largely left to unionism's own intramural devices, in the USA the whole matter had to be handed over to a central government authority.

Yet such considerations do not wholly satisfy our curiosity about the political aspect of American labour. We would expect that in any industrialized nation that is also a democracy, economic differences, however narrow their scope, would impel the contestants toward political confrontation more persistent and formalized than has been the American experience. A more elementary approach may yield greater understanding. Politics involves demands made in particular ways and in particular expectations. These expectations are never a 'given' thing, but vary with times and circumstances. To understand the attitude of American workers towards politics at any historical juncture, therefore, we must know what their expectations were and what means, political or apolitical, they considered most appropriate for realizing them.

Up until some point in the latter half of the nineteenth century these expectations knew no bounds. The New World's abundant and varied natural resources, its ever-receding horizon of opportunity in an ever-expanding market protected by external tariff walls, drew the settler on. A seemingly inexhaustible supply of land, which was not (as in Australia) locked up by the government in great holdings, but free or cheap and lacking only the men to work it, put labour at a premium. While historians are divided as to the 'safety-valve' function of the frontier, we need not doubt that every worker who passed through to the public domain of the West improved the bargaining-power of the residue of skilled labour in the East by preserving its scarcity.

Thus circumstanced, generations of American workers could believe their expectations fulfillable within the framework of life they found. This contained few reminders of the social order they had left: physically, no castles, guildhalls or manor houses; legally, no primogeniture and entail, and no successful indenturing of servants. Away from the established cities of the East there existed no considerable social stratification; outside the Southern plantations, no landed gentry. There was no firmly entrenched and privileged social order to be broken down or into *pour mêler les fortunes*, no customary living standards to be observed. His very reasons for emigrating made the worker unlikely to wish to re-create the social features he had left behind. So long as American society appeared one undifferentiated middle class there could be no fixed and depressed class of wage-earners looking to the state for emancipation. With the rise of the merchant capitalists in the 1820s, driven by mutual competition to keep wage costs down, a distinction between employer and employee status did indeed begin to emerge. But it long remained fluid enough to leave the latter an incentive to demolish the obstacles to himself becoming a small capitalist. And a workers' party could not stabilize itself so long as its nucleus, the skilled journeymen, believed they had a chance to set up their own shops and become employers. The worker's belief that he was free to rise as far as his own abilities, resources and luck could take him persisted long. As late as the 1880s the Knights of Labour were holding out the prospect of 'a system of co-operation which will eventually make every man his own master, every man his own employer'.

There was no reason why means to such an end should not include political action, for universal male franchise was early approached by most American state constitutions. The forces that swept Andrew Jackson to the Presidency in 1828 were to bring the vote to most men of little or no property. But in practice the means chosen by early workers' combinations varied with their estimate of what offered at any juncture the best means – political action, co-operatives of producers or consumers, free land or cheap money – of realizing their ambition to escape their lot as workers. It was a question as to which immediate obstacle – the monopolist, the land-grabber, the 'money power' – was to be removed from their path to individual proprietorship. Some of their political demands – such as the ten-hour day (introduced in 1840 by President Van Buren into 'all public establishments') and a mechanics' lien law – were naturally peculiar to their category as workers. But with these went demands for the removal of general hindrances to self-advancement – for universal free education, the abolition of all chartered monopolies, free access to land for individual settlers (in the 1840s) and then (in the 1860s) the credit necessary to work it.

The same circumstances, however, which encouraged individual expectations did not necessarily favour co-operative group action for realizing them. If class did not divide, neither did it unify. Individual insecurity in the presence of the means of unlimited accumulation bred intolerance and violence. Each new wave of immigrants – the whole constituting a folk-movement unique in history – added to the diversity of languages and backgrounds among the labour force, elicited the hostility of established workers who feared (not without justification) their use to undercut wage rates or break strikes, and allowed conservative elements to stigmatize collectivist political doctrines of any kind as the symptom of imperfect Americanization. Andrew Carnegie, himself a Scot by birth, called American socialists 'a parcel of foreign cranks whose communistic ideas [are] the natural growth of unjust laws of their native land'. Continuous expansion of the labour market meant that no 'national' labour movement could remain national for long. The prospect of free land ('Vote Yourself a Farm') for the claiming, while stimulating the quest for proprietorship, encouraged the prospector to be ever on the move, resulting in continuous dislocation of the working force. It disinclined the individual to subordinate his own prospects to any concept of a communal good, while predisposing him fiercely to the defence of property rights, whether against his employer, his employees, or later arrivals to the work force. Above all, early enfranchisement deprived American workers of the one common objective which in Britain propelled every type of labourer into political engagement, with all its solidifying effects.

For these reasons early workingmen's parties, such as those formed in the late 1820s in Philadelphia, New York and Connecticut, were transient phenomena. They disappeared with the return of prosperity, if they had not meanwhile succumbed to denunciation as 'workeyism' from the 'respectable' public, or to the embrace of the Jacksonian Democrats or their opponents. Few local labour organizations survived the depression of 1837, and only three considerable trade unions (by then of 'national' scope) weathered the great panic of twenty years later. It was more normal for such combinations to pursue their ends through existing parties; and indeed most of the workingmen's demands of those years, translated into Locofoco principles, were to occupy the Democratic party until the Civil War. But other movements, too, absorbed workers' energies in their attempt to escape the wage system. During the 1840s the hopes of many from land reform drew them toward George Henry Evans's National Reform Association, which in the following decade merged into the homestead movement of the

Republican party. The expedient of producers' co-operatives was tried again in the 1850s and 1860s, and was returned to periodically thereafter. A great variety of secular associationist communities were started up in widely different areas: all foundered on the individual desire to become a capitalist.

Sometimes mechanics combined with the unskilled and the farmers, as in Massachusetts in the early 1830s. But the first multi-purpose workers' movement of size and note was the National Labour Union of 1866. Its miscellany of objectives included some defensive of labour organizations: – the affiliation of all skills and of the unskilled too, provision for the voluntary arbitration of disputes, an end to the truck system of wage payment, abolition of convict labour and suspension of Chinese labouring immigration (the latter not attained until 1882, and then largely through the efforts of Californian workers). Other goals repeated general specifics: producers' co-operatives and reservation of the public domain to individual settlers. But to these was added a new demand – for the eight-hour working day. It was long to remain in the forefront of labour platforms: for, though Congress duly enacted a federal eight-hour law in 1868, employers, including at first the federal government itself, insisted on reducing wages correspondingly.

The other novelty adopted by the National Labour Union was a variation on a plan for currency reform earlier put forward by one Edward Kellogg. In the hope of relieving a monetary scarcity allegedly caused by the policy of private banks, and particularly to enable co-operatives to obtain capital more cheaply, the Union called on government to dismantle the national banking system, and to lend paper money (issued on a basis of real estate) directly to citizens at a very low fixed rate of interest. 'Abolition of the wage system' was once again the goal. Over this policy of Greenbackism (as it was called) the National Labour Union's 1870 congress split, one section adopting the name of Labour Reform party, and being taken over almost at once by Democrats or anti-Grant Republicans, while the centre of interest in Greenbackism proper moved westward to the predominantly farming region of the upper Mississippi valley. In only a small part of this area did its 1880 Presidential candidate pick up labour votes in any significant quantity. For the city labour elements came to look doubtfully upon the inflationary consequence of currency reform, which for the agrarians was its main attraction.

Greenback-labour parties continued for a time on state bases, often in alliance with the Democrats but sometimes as independent organizations. A notable example of the latter type was the party formed in Massachusetts by the Knights of St Crispin (shoemakers), whose platform added to the National Labour Union's a call for the establishment of a bureau of labour statistics. Massachusetts responded by creating in 1870 the first such invaluable repository of information. Here at least was one permanent institutional gain to survive the disastrous depression of 1873, which left only seven unions standing. General collapse of the economy, beginning with the banking house of Jay Cooke & Co., spread a trail of ruin where one-fifth of the country's workforce was unemployed and the remainder on greatly reduced wages. It touched off also that appalling sequence of violent episodes collectively known as the Railway strike of 1877. As for political parties, their organization shrank back to a city base.

One last attempt was to be made, and that the most ambitious, to sweep together all members of the 'producing classes' of America, including women and Negroes, into a single mass movement. The Knights of Labour, a semi-occult and ritualist association originally the offshoot of a Philadelphia garment workers' local, had for its express aim the harmonization of labour and capital through co-operative institutions, both productive and distributive, in every branch of industry. After ten years of slow growth it could make some claim to be a national organization by the time its 1878 convention, at Reading, Pennsylvania, adopted a platform which summed up most of labour's political demands of the previous and succeeding decades. This advocated voluntary arbitration of disputes; an effectual eight-hour day; prohibition of convict and oriental labour; abolition of the contract system on public works; legislation to protect the labourer's health and safety; equal pay for equal work; the banning from industry of children under fourteen years; establishment of postal savings banks; government ownership of railroads, telegraphs and telephones; and withal, equality for both labour and capital in the eyes of the law.

Membership of the Order remained for several years unstable: partly because of the vacillations of its head, Terence Powderley, towards strikes and independent political engagement (nationally the Knights' preference was for Washington lobbying); partly because, sympathetic to industrial unionization rather than to craft, it suffered a high turnover of unskilled enrolment. The depression of 1883, however, and the great wave of strikes in its train, swelled numbers to 100,000 by 1885 and to 700,000 by 1886. Alarmed at this mushrooming of the unskilled element with its uncontrollable passions, Powderley drew the Knights back from the eight-hour campaign at a critical point. Then came the bomb explosion during a demonstration in Haymarket Square, Chicago, on the night of 4 May 1886. The police retaliated with rifle fire, the courts with judicial revenge upon eight scapegoats.

The main consequences of the Haymarket affair were twofold. On the one hand, a virulent anti-labour campaign ran through courts, legislatures and the public, to which last the incident appeared as the climax of ten years of mounting violence. On the other hand, because this setback was not an economic one but social and political, unionism did not this time retreat, as it had in earlier bad times, into the refuge of producers' co-operatives, but closed its ranks politically in self-defence. In New York more than 150 labour organizations united around the banner of Progressive Democracy held aloft by the great single-taxer, Henry George. His mayoralty candidature failing – many of the ballots cast proved untraceable at the counting stage – his left-wing supporters hived off to form a Progressive Labour party. The residue undauntedly rechristened themselves United Labour. Neither prospered in the New York state elections of 1887. Although better fortune attended United Labour (or Union Labour) parties in Chicago, Cleveland, Milwaukee and a number of seaboard states from Massachusetts to Virginia, the effort to unite these movements in time for the 1888 national elections failed, and with it the last important nation-wide political movement of workers in nineteenth-century America.

The mid-1880s mark a parting of the ways in American labour's history which carried certain important implications for its politics. By the end of that decade the spread of railroads and other communications across the continent were making the market a truly national one. Few men henceforward could seriously continue to harbour the belief in an unlimited opportunity to rise out of the wage-earning category. At a juncture when immigration was approaching its peak, unionists and non-unionists had to come to grips with industrial powers that had by now so consolidated their position as to be almost impregnable. Labour, on the contrary, had found no secure basis from which to grapple with a nascent business corporatism. At no level – national, state or even city – had it been able to shape a durable political organization through which to mitigate the effects of industrial depressions, every one of which since 1837 had left a promising union movement either crushed or badly retarded. Violence was reaching its zenith. The Homestead and Pullman strikes lay just ahead, together with the first great period of the federal labour injunction as an employers' weapon. By then the vistas of boundless opportunity would have clouded over to the point where the militant organizer of the American Railroad Union, Eugene V. Debs, declared the Homestead strikers 'content if they could build for themselves humble homes, obtain the necessaries of life, rear their children as becomes American citizens, and save a few dollars for a "rainy day", and secure for themselves a decent burial'. In 1893, the word 'unemployment' made its début in Noah Webster's book of terms. Much of the labour force was to continue to let itself be diverted into a variety of political and economic expedients. Agrarian protest, though its numerical strength was on the wane, could do more than flicker for some decades to come. Farmer-labour-co-operative parties still had some part to play. Yet by the mid-eighties economic specialization had reached the point where urban wage-earners could no longer plausibly identify themselves in outlook, interest or action with other American producing classes.

One section of the work force to read the new signs were the skilled craftsmen. A group of these seceded from the Knights of Labour in Indiana in 1881 to help form a Federation of Organized Trades and Labour Unions, a body wherein the skilled would enjoy, if not exclusive membership, at any rate exclusive control. It was by no means apolitical. Three years later, though small, it was taking the lead in the eight-hour movement. Towards it gravitated the Cigarmakers union, with Samuel Gompers among its chief officers, in the course of resisting raids by the Knights upon certain of its locals. After negotiations with the Order had failed to give craft unions adequate security, the Federation at its 1886 convention took to itself independence and the title of American Federation of Labour (AFL). Deserted on the other side by the unskilled, the Knights during the 1890s virtually merged into the Northern and Southern Alliances of agrarians, and what effective influence it still possessed flowed out into the sea of Populism.

At the head of the new Federation, Gompers fought off pressures, from the Knights to include the unskilled, and from the Socialists to support radical and independent political ventures. Instead he offered an alternative course (whose effects the following chapter will more fully explore) which came to be known as voluntarism – a doctrine that saw unionism as one of the natural forms of voluntary association among men, with the same claim as any other association to autonomy and freedom from the intervention of government. The latter's role should be peripheral, confined to enabling unions to compete with employers on roughly equal terms. Government should protect the unionist against unfair competition in the labour market (by restricting immigration, banning competitive convict labour, and so on) and might minimally improve the condition of those regarded as unorganizable. But it was for the unions, in the first instance, to provide unemployment relief for their members. As late as 1930 Gompers's successor was stigmatizing unemployment insurance as 'unfair, discriminatory and unscientific'. Gompers himself used language almost identical with the judiciary's in opposing a legal minimum wage for women as 'a curb upon the rights and . . . opportunity of development of the women employed in the industries of our country'. Nor *a fortiori* was it the business of any legislature to restrict the freedom either of the union to strike or of the employer to fire men at will.

So low an estimate of the value of government for fulfilling workers' expectations could in the 1880s claim the virtue of realism. The American political process was, and remains, highly fragmented. For much of the nineteenth century, concentrations of working men were sparsely distributed and in

no position decisively to influence state governments, still less
the federal. Representation in legislatures at both levels was,
and so continued till the redistricting of the 1960s, distinctly
biassed towards the thinly-populated rural areas unresponsive
to the needs of the cities. And in any case the favours most
often sought by unions were local ones – from the city hall or
the police. Government, moreover, and especially the federal
government, was for decades an extraneous factor in American
industrial life, intrinsically incapable of implementing a con-
sistent economic policy. Before 1912 there existed very little
public law in the country's economic affairs, but rather a network of self-governing economic enclaves. What would it have
availed labour to press a general social or economic platform
upon Washington?

Furthermore, any progressive measures passed through the
legislature had to run the gauntlet of the courts. These have
always in the USA been more thinly insulated from politics,
from the prevailing social *mores* and business climate, than in
most democracies. After the Civil War they shared the almost
universal reluctance to see obstacles placed in the path of the
country's rapid industrialization. For more than half a century
judges were assiduous in defending the employer's property
interest in his business by protecting his freedom of action, and
that of the evolving business corporation, against harassment
by trade unions.

In 1842 an American state court for the first time allowed
(in *Commonwealth v. Hunt*) that combination of workmen to
raise wages was not *per se* unlawful. But this principle soon
became overlaid with the question of the legality of the union's
methods and objectives. Without conscious anti-labour bias,
upholding freedom of contract, and in the name of a public good
which required that commerce be unobstructed, judges applied
the English common law doctrine of conspiracy in restraint of
trade to the conditions of the modern industrial state, for which
it had never been designed. If they did not precisely deny the
right of workers to bargain collectively, they often made imprac-
ticable the only means of asserting this right. While leaving the
employer free to use his defensive armoury – the 'yellow dog'
contract (a compulsory undertaking from the employee, without reciprocal benefit to himself, not to join a union: *Anglice*,

'the document'), discriminatory discharge and secret black-listing, the use of strikebreakers, spies and provocateurs – they forbade the union to wield its own peculiar offensive weapons of the strike, the sympathetic strike ('secondary boycott') and picketing. 'There can be no such thing as peaceful picketing,' said a court flatly as late as 1905.

During the early years of the AFL, common law as an anti-union instrument was yielding pride of place to damage and anti-trust suits under statutory provision, and above all to that very handy and speedy device applied at the employer's request, the injunction restraining a union from activities allegedly injurious to his business. This judicial threat to unions persisted in despite of the clear findings of successive US Industrial Commissions, and special commissions appointed to look into major strikes, who from 1880 to 1902 repeatedly exposed the true facts of the labour-management relationship and urged adoption of the more rational attitudes that had come to prevail in Great Britain.

Throughout this period, too, the courts consistently interpreted Congress's power to tax or to regulate interstate commerce, together with the police power of the states, so as to invalidate many attempts of government to shape and apply ameliorative social legislation such as might ease the labourer's hours and conditions of work or ensure him a minimum wage or insurance against his old age. In 1913 a much-travelled American labour leader reckoned that in provisions for workmen's compensation his country was still ten years behind Britain, twenty behind Germany. Small wonder that European visitors of the early twentieth century castigated Americans for their 'social irresponsibility', and even as late as the 1920s brought back horror stories of child employment.

Since throughout most of the nineteenth century American government was neither responsive to labour's needs nor susceptible to its control, it appeared only reasonable that leaders like Gompers should view its operations with more apprehension than hope. Even when the faith of *laisser-faire* was being roundly contradicted by the facts of economic life, many unionists preferred to further their expectations by organizing their own control over the conditions of their job by direct economic pressure upon the employer.

Nevertheless it was in the long run unfortunate that Gompersian voluntarism became so soon frozen into the official creed of the AFL. For out of the turbulent 1890s began to emerge greater promise and potentiality of the state as instrument of its citizens' welfare. The magnitude of this change can best be appreciated when looked back on from the year 1917. By the time the USA entered the First World War, almost all its states possessed labour departments and permanent boards of industrial arbitration. All had factory inspection laws; thirty provided voluntary insurance schemes against industrial accidents, and a beginning had been made in employers' liability and workmen's compensation. Nearly every state forbade the employment in industry or services of children under fourteen years; four-fifths prescribed maximum hours, and a dozen laid down minimum wage rates, for women in industry. The first state ten-hour law had been upheld by the Supreme Court, and the maximal eight-hour day established on the railroads. Of these last, the Court had significantly declared that the railway owners had 'devoted their property to public use and must therefore consent to be regulated by the legislature representing the public'.

In sum these gains amounted to the enactment of most, though not all, of the Progressive party's platform of 1912. Since that platform drew upon the programme not only of ex-Populists but of the Socialist party also, it is fitting that the latter's contribution should be, however summarily, examined at this point.

Socialist influence in America has been continuous since 1865, when Lassalleans founded their German Workingmen's Union in New York city and tried to penetrate the National Labour Union. Like the labour movement as a whole, socialism in America was to attempt every expedient indifferently – the ballot box or trade unionism, independent party activity or boring other organizations from within, and 'direct' action, violent or otherwise. After the First International transferred its seat to New York in 1872 the movement was long rent with internal conflicts, not all of them doctrinal, but most polarized between that city and Chicago. Its most prominent figure in the 1890s was Daniel De Leon, who rose to power through his editorship of the Socialist Labour party's newspaper. Attempting to capture the Knights of Labour, he succeeded in having

Powderley unseated, only to be ousted himself. From his base in the Jewish needle trades of New York, De Leon summoned all dedicated workers to the class struggle, to war on both the Knights and the AFL, and in 1896 to support of its own independent Presidential ticket.

By then a number of dissenters had withdrawn to follow Victor Berger, a Marxist whose advocacy of a more realistic scale of political engagement was yielding some success in Milwaukee and Chicago. In 1896 Berger was joined by Debs, and the group took the title of Social Democrats. When the Socialist Labour party at its 1900 convention followed De Leon in abjuring pure-and-simple trade unionism in favour of the complete overthrow of the wage system, the rival, essentially trade unionist, wing of the party under Morris Hillquit followed the earlier seceders to support a Debs-Hillquit national ticket. It attracted nearly 100,000 votes; and the Hillquitters then formally united with the Social Democrats to form the Socialist Party of America, dedicated to ultimate achievement of a socialist society through independent political action. Meanwhile its immediate goals were state regulation of trusts, mines, transport and communications; shorter hours of work; abolition of child labour; a graduated income tax and the initiative and referendum – programmatically the equivalent (one might say) of the left wing of the Progressive party.

Between 1901 and 1904 the Socialist party's membership had doubled to 2,000, incorporating men and women from almost every walk of life, and in the latter year Debs's candidature for the US Presidency drew some 420,000 votes. The party's 'good government' appeal was particularly strong at the municipal level: the one thousand of its members holding public office in 1912 included (beside one Congressman – Debs) no fewer than fifty-six mayors. At the same time its boring-from-within tactics in the AFL, a number of whose leaders were themselves ex-Socialists, sorely worried Gompers. In 1902 the party came within 800 votes of carrying the Federation's national convention into independent political action, and at its 1912 convention the Socialist rival for Gompers's presidential chair received one-third of all votes cast.

Though the party was to flourish for another five years, 1912 was the high water mark of socialism in the United States.

From the country's entry into World War I it declined, for reasons which were not merely to do with national security. In the New World it had not escaped the inherent dilemmas that racked it in Europe: whether as to ends – revolution or evolution? or as to means – purity or compromise with non-socialists? It displayed in its new habitat the same amoeba-like propensity for dividing and subdividing. But in addition the transatlantic climate was more inhospitable. Even doctrinal rebels have rarely challenged the fundamental tenets of American capitalism. Jack London may have marched with Kelley's Army of the unemployed, but he also planned to build himself the most palatial ranch-house in the West. There is nothing socialistic about the Utopian prophecies of Edward Bellamy and his like. Though socialism and other reforming creeds for decades had access to some five-sixths of the organizable workers of the United States, they rarely managed to inspire them with a divine discontent. Indeed, they themselves did not escape contagion. 'To this day', wrote Trotsky in 1930,

> I smile as I recall the leaders of American socialism.
> Immigrants who had played some role in Europe in their
> youth, they very quickly lost the theoretical premise they had
> brought with them in the confusion of their struggle for
> success.

Immigrant ex-Socialists provided the conservative AFL with many of its early leaders. The *International Socialist Review*, which banished Werner Sombart from its pages for having declared that the American worker 'is not in any way antagonistic to the capitalist economic system as such ... indeed, I believe he likes it,' itself carried advertisements for gold-mine shares, Florida land, and Doubling or Trebling Your Money by Clean Honest Investment. A Los Angeles boulevard immortalizes the name of one 'millionaire socialist': another a few years ago ran under that title for the mayoralty of New York.

It is remarkable that the New World, while giving refuge to social and political innovators of all kinds, has given credence to so few. Hawthorne was voicing the opinions of more than the tough-minded Jacksonians when he asserted that 'no sagacious man will long retain his sagacity if he live exclusively among reformers and progressive people'. Upton Sinclair, after twenty years of evangelizing, concluded that socialism was eccentric to the American middle-class mentality. Too often the intellectual in politics has been associated in the American mind with unconformable dilettantism, feminism, 'sexual novelties', and a universal language. It is significant that the first American appearance of the complete Communist Manifesto in English should have been in a periodical devoted to 'universological science' and edited by two eccentric sisters, who both eventually married safely and well into the English aristocracy.

Socialism, said William Graham Sumner, 'is any device or doctrine whose aim is to save individuals from any of the difficulties or hardships of the struggle for existence and the competition of life by the intervention of "the State" '. Certainly it ran, in both its communism and its statism, clean contrary to the fierce native attachment to private property and enterprise. Its class basis contradicted the all-inclusive American ethos: to embrace socialism would be to confess that the melting-pot had failed. The determinist materialism of Marx denied the optimistic, pragmatic materialism of the expanding republic. Americans were prone to view it as an exotic, its ready-made doctrines and vocabulary as relevant only to Europe, and its leaders, even when American-born, as spiritual aliens. Norman Thomas was not to be hailed as 'a great American' before his seventieth birthday, by when the movement he led had long been considered harmless. At its best electoral showing of recent decades, in 1948, Thomas polled not much better than the Prohibitionist candidate – less than three-tenths of 1 % of all votes cast.

At a period, however, when to its alien doctrines it coupled practical violence, a socialist movement could alert the entire American middle-class in favour of its suppression. Out of the financial panic of 1893 and the following depression arose in the Rocky Mountain states the Western Federation of Miners, to seek the eight-hour day for mine, mill and smelter workers by methods of frontier lawlessness which provoked retaliation equally brutal. When in 1905 they entered the International Workers of the World ('the Wobblies'), the Socialist party withdrew to a distance. The lurid activities of the Wobblies over the next ten years, involving the trial and acquittal of their leader 'Big Bill' Haywood after the murder of an ex-governor of Idaho, have concealed the simple and concrete nature of their objectives, which were little more than higher wages and shorter hours. By publicly revealing the deplorable working conditions among agricultural and lumber workers (whom they alone succeeded in organizing), the IWW contributed a certain animus to progressive movements. It was a one-time Wobbly, William Z. Foster, who directed the AFL's organizing drives of 1918 in the steel industry.

Once America had begun to wage world war, left-wing movements of every kind suffered in varying degrees under the Espionage and Sedition Acts of 1917 and 1918. The Wobblies faced extermination. The Socialists, whose convention had voted against belligerency and military conscription, endured raids, prosecutions and the conviction of their leaders. With peace came the aftermath, the Red Scare of 1919, intensified by the high predominance of Slavs among recent pre-war immigration. At its 1920 convention the right wing of the Socialist party, which largely controlled its machinery, prudently secured rejection of a motion to affiliate with the Third International, and again nominated Debs (now in prison) as its Presidential candidate. The party's left wing seceded only to split still further, the irreconcilables among them going on to form the Communist Labour party and to avow their goal to be the dictatorship of the proletariat – a step which enabled the authorities and the public at large henceforth to label all labour militance as 'Bolshevik'. In many states communists and socialists were prosecuted and gaoled, and everywhere suspected radicals were being rounded up. The New York state Assembly ruled five Socialists (including Hillquit) ineligible to take their seats, and Congress twice expelled Berger. The federal government used its powers to deport, sometimes *en masse*, until at the height of the scare, in January 1920, the Secretary of Labour felt obliged to declare that in his view the Communist party was not an illegal organization. It nevertheless went underground, to re-emerge at the end of the following year as the Workers Party of America: by 1923 it was being entirely directed from Moscow. Since Congress in 1940 proscribed any group that advocates the overthrow of any government in the USA by force, the party has been harried by both legislative and executive branches of government, and its plight has been only partially relieved by the courts.

Too much stress, however, upon the incompatibility of socialism as a non-indigenous ideology may obscure the practical and institutional handicaps under which, as a party, it labours in the USA, and which it shares with any American labour movement resorting to independent political action. The two great American parties historically precede the rise of industrial labour, command deep-rooted personal and family loyalties, and display a remarkable elasticity in adapting themselves so as to absorb the programme and the votes of protest movements. Being non-doctrinal, they are instruments of consensus rather than of choice, mobilizers of heterogeneous majorities, possessing a vitality and resilience which it is foolish to underestimate. Their platforms are not crusading banners but compromise agreements, their politicians more concerned to satisfy local or regional interests than to implement a centrally-devised programme. Policies are made, not in the party conclave, nor in the polling booths, but in the legislative halls.

Hence the quandary of any labour or socialist movement. While virtually every Presidential election since the Civil War has seen the appearance of one or more minor parties, not one of them has transformed itself into a major. It has no loaves and fishes of patronage to offer. Even if a third party can succeed in getting itself on the ballot in a majority of states, it will suffer from the winner-take-all, first-past-the-post, electoral system of most American constituencies. Third-party action is therefore to be regarded as the last, desperate resort of a neglected group in order to bring its grievances and voting power to the attention of a major party. Even if it were possible to identify beyond a limited range of issues a truly labour platform, yet of all groups labour could least afford to draw upon itself the collective wrath of the middle class – that 'most terrible and implacable force', as William Morris called it. Socialists in particular have learnt that the party which is unequivocally doctrinaire is incurably weak, dooming itself to remain outside the political mainstream.

To overcome this impotence and isolation, periodic attempts have been made by various discontented groups to combine in support of a joint ticket. But socialist-labour is an unstable compound. Until recent years trade unions have not seen them-

selves as vehicles of social reform, still less of social revolution.
On its most impressive showing in 1912 – still only 6% of the
popular vote – the Socialist party scored better in predominantly
rural states (such as Oklahoma) than in the most heavily
industrialized. By their actions some of its leaders have tended,
like De Leon, to drive a wedge between themselves and organized
labour. Radical union officers in America, unlike Hardie,
Smillie or Mann in Britain, have left the party in despair, while
their rank-and-file have viewed the 'campus intellectual' with
mistrust. Nor have farmer-labourer alliances been comfortable
for long. Farmers have sought low freight rates, railroad
unionists higher pay: the farmer wants high prices for agricultural products and low for machinery, *vice versa* the urban
worker.

The last third party to receive even the grudging endorsement
of the AFL was in fact a miscellany of railroad workers,
Socialists, the Farmer-Labour party of Minnesota, and a
number of socio-political groups. In dissatisfaction with the
major parties' candidates and attitudes, these came together in
1923 under the label of Progressive in support of the Presidential
candidacy of Robert M. LaFollette of Wisconsin. Their platform was the by now familiar anti-monopoly one, demanding
state ownership of the nation's reserves of water and oil,
redistribution of taxation in favour of the individual worker and
farmer, reduction in tariffs and in railway rates, and banning of
the injunction from labour disputes and of all children from
industry. After some organizational difficulties, eased somewhat
by taking advantage of the Socialist party machinery already
existing in 44 states, the Progressives in 1924 polled nearly 17%
of the vote, capturing Wisconsin and showing strength in
Illinois, Ohio, Pennsylvania and New York. Though it helped
return twenty Congressmen and six Senators to Washington, the
alliance was not cohesive enough long to survive the campaign.
It acted as a temporary spur to those union leaders in the AFL
concerned to do something for the rising number of unorganized
industrial workers. But its chief legislative memorial was the
Railroad Labour Act of 1926, which brought permanent federal
mediation machinery into a strike-torn public service.

Looking back over a long succession of disappointments,
American labour has learnt to regard third-party activity,

whether on its own or in alliance with other dissatisfied elements, as a policy of last resort. Now and again, even today, an officer of a temporarily aggrieved international (i.e., a component union of the AFL, so called because it may have some members outside the USA) will argue a case for such a course during an AFL–CIO convention. But unionism normally prefers to bargain with an existing party from outside, and where possible to exert pressure in collusion with other like-minded groups from issue to issue. The limited way in which labour exercised this non-partisanship under Gompers is examined in the following chapter. His view that, with only rare electoral interventions, unionism could be left to work out with business the country's economic salvation was finally effaced by the catastrophe of 1929. The New Deal, by bringing the federal government unprecedented economic influence (studied in Chapter 3), correspondingly magnified its capacity for fulfilling labour's expectations. At the same time it transformed the judiciary from an obstacle in the unions' path into their ally. How they thereafter enlarged and formalized their machinery for continuous political intervention, normally on behalf of the Democrats, is considered in Chapter 4: how they used it to mitigate the conservative reaction following World War II will appear from Chapter 5.

Today the federal government is not only itself the biggest American employer, but undertakes the task of regulating the total volume of national employment. Its actions, rather than the mutual manoeuvrings of unions and management, determine the worker's conditions of life. Nevertheless, its social legislation, though considerable, is for the unionist overshadowed in importance by its control of the labour-management relationship. In this control the American public at large, too, have an interest. Are American unions, anti-competitive institutions in a competitive environment, bound to produce inflationary consequences? Will the movement that found its feet in the 1880s be as revolutionary in its consequences as it is conservative in its intentions? We touch, in conclusion, on these questions. For, as labour is well aware, they will be answered not in the economic sphere but in the political.

2

The voluntarism of Samuel Gompers

The only American labour movement with claims to longevity is inseparably bound up with the man who led it for more than forty years. Samuel Gompers, born in 1850 to Dutch-Jewish parents in a Spitalfields tenement, arrived at the age of thirteen in New York. On its East Side he rose to office in his Cigarmakers Union, became in 1881 chairman of the Federation of Organised Trade and Labour Unions (FOTLU), and in 1886 a co-founder of its successor, the American Federation of Labour. Thereafter, for thirty-seven years all save one, he remained the AFL's president and personification.

Gompers in his early working years was intimate with a group of European refugees, some of whom had been members of the First International and others direct disciples of Marx. By them he was introduced to the tenets of revolutionary Marxism, some of which were duly embodied in the preamble to the constitution of FOTLU and were to remain, however incongruously, with only slight modification until 1955 the constitutional preamble of the AFL itself:

> A struggle is going on in all the nations of the civilized world between the oppressors and oppressed in all countries, a struggle between capital and labour, which must grow in intensity from year to year and work disastrous results to the toiling millions of all nations if not combined for mutual protection and benefit.

Indeed, traces of Marx's economism and universalism were to persist throughout Gompers's own writings:

> The emancipation of labour is neither a local nor a national but a social problem embracing all countries in which modern society exists (1875).

> Economic power is the basis upon which may be developed power in other fields. It is the foundation of organised society. Whoever or whatever controls economic power directs and shapes development for the group or the nation. Economic law and necessity are stronger than legislative or police power (1914).

> The concept that economic organization and control over economic power were the fulcrum which made possible influence and power in all other fields [was the] fundamental concept upon which the American Federation of Labour was later developed . . . The secret of this continuous progress has been understanding of the nature and possibilities of economic power, and concentration on mobilization of that power (1923).

Contact with the American environment, however, led Gompers and his associates before long to doubt the relevance of Marxism *pure et dure* to labour's transatlantic circumstances, and to insist upon 'the necessity for an American movement under American control'. The result was to be a movement which, retaining much of Marx's economic analysis yet almost none of his ideology, has appeared an almost unique phenomenon – a kind of conservative syndicalism.

First and foremost, it affirmed (1890) that 'the trade unions, pure and simple, are the natural organizations of the wage earners to secure their present material and practical improvement and to achieve their final emancipation'. The young Federation officially declined all alliances with non-union groups, whether farmers, radical ideologues, populists or intellectuals, and held aloof from any notion of 'one big union' of all 'the producing classes'. Within its conventions Gompers waged 'a fight to a finish' against the Socialist element. From

British unionism the AFL determined to copy only its service side – the Cigarmakers' insurance system was a conscious imitation of that of the Amalgamated Engineers – and deliberately to eschew the political example of Henry Broadhurst and the parliamentary committee of the TUC.

The AFL, child of depression, would make virtues of its limitations. It would base itself upon the market value of skilled craft labour, excluding the unskilled by high initiation fees and long apprenticeship. It would fight all 'dual' unionism and recognize a charter from the Federation as the sole badge of a union's legitimacy. Acknowledging the autonomy of each skill, it would be content to remain a loose confederation of craft unions, each respecting the other's peculiar structures and jurisdictional rights. The AFL's national executive (of which the president was until 1891 the only full-time officer) would enjoy only such powers as its component unions would concede to it: Gompers in 1912 cited the federal government of the USA as an analogy, but in truth the kingdom of Poland would have been a better one. What bound the aristocracy of American labour together was 'at once a rope of sand and yet the strongest human force – a voluntary association united by common need and held together by mutual self-interest'.

For the foreseeable future unionism must accept and work within a system of *laisser-faire* capitalism, and strive to obtain for skilled workers an increasing share of its fruits. 'The American Federation of Labour,' declared its first president, 'stands squarely and unequivocally for the defence and maintenance of the existing order,' and would extend no help to those who wished to reform it by governmental regulation or otherwise. 'I had no quarrel with large scale organization,' wrote Gompers, 'I am not going to join in the howl against trusts; all I ask is to give us the freedom we want to work our own salvation and to give industry the same opportunity.' The bigger the system, the bigger labour's stake in it.

From this system it was the mission of 'business unionism' to wrest 'more, here and now'. The American surrogate for Marxian revolution was to be permanent revolution in the worker's economic status by piecemeal but continuous pressure on owner-management, exerted through his own institutions. But 'we have no ultimate ends. We are going on from day to

3

day.' An open-ended goal was to be pursued through an infinite and inexhaustible series of 'immediate demands'. This doctrine was even more explicitly stated by Gompers in the course of a long duel with the socialist Hillquit before the US Commission on Industrial Relations of 1912:

GOMPERS   The best possible conditions obtainable for the workers is the aim.

HILLQUIT   Yes, and when these conditions are obtained –

GOMPERS   Why, then we want better.

HILLQUIT   Now, my question is – Will this effort on the part of organized labour ever stop until it has the full reward for its labour?

GOMPERS   It won't stop at all.

HILLQUIT   That is a question –

GOMPERS   Not when any particular point is reached . . . The working people will never stop –

HILLQUIT   Exactly –

GOMPERS   in their efforts to obtain a better life for themselves and for their wives and for their children and for humanity . . . it is the effort to obtain a better life every day.

HILLQUIT   Every day and always?

GOMPERS   Every day. That does not limit it.

HILLQUIT   Until such time? –

GOMPERS   Not until any time.

HILLQUIT   In other words –

GOMPERS   In other words, we go further than you. (*Laughter and applause in the audience.*) You have an end. We have not.

Herein lay the solution of the paradox which so perplexed European visitors to the United States of seventy years ago. The American industrial conflict was no less bitter for being fought over the distribution of benefits accruing from a system which both contestants accepted. Indeed, the very absence of political pre-occupations sharpened the contest in that the worker saw his mode of life as directly and solely related to the terms he could wring from his employer, who alone stood between him and 'the earth and the fulness thereof'. The unions, by exercise of what is nowadays fashionable to call counter-vailing power, fought management for control over the conditions and fruits of production, though without any intention of using that control to revise economic fundamentals. No programme better fitted its environment. So long as natural resources were regarded as limitless, its objectives did not seem incongruent with the democratic climate in which they were pursued. Labour's sanguineness about the future was perfectly attuned to the expectations of nineteenth-century liberal capitalism and American society as a whole: and since it asked no more of the future than did any other social or economic groups, its claims were no less reasonable than theirs. Gompers might therefore hope to reassure the great American middle class of property owners that these claims, being compatible with any other group's, and realizable without radical trans-formation of the existing social structure, should be tolerated.

What room did this approach leave for political action? We noted earlier some general circumstances making it unlikely that organized labour in nineteenth-century America could expect to achieve much from political engagement above the purely local level. There were additional reasons why Gompers was pessimistic about the value of politicians and government to his young movement. There were, for instance, labour's past disappointments, such as the failure of the eight-hour-day bill Andrew Johnson had signed into law in 1868. Shorter hours had in practice meant lower wages. Gompers's own Cigarmakers Union had helped secure from the New York state legislature a statute forbidding the 'putting-out system', whereby cigars were made in private homes, only to see it invalidated by the courts: the union had eventually succeeded only through economic pressure upon the employers.

At a deeper level, there was inherent in his Marxian econo-mism the *a priori* assumption that political agencies at most merely registered the outcome of economic conflicts which they were powerless to control:

Organization was response to economic forces, and therefore I did not believe that arbitrary limitations especially by law could prevail against it . . . The state is not capable of preventing the development or the natural concentration of industry, and all propositions to that purpose react for the greater injury to wage earners than to trusts. Several times the plain question has been put to me by members of the Senate committee on Judiciary: 'Mr Gompers, what can we do to allay the causes of strikes that bring discomfort and financial suffering to all alike?' I have had to answer 'Nothing'. It is difficult for lawyers to understand that the most important human justice comes through other agencies than the political. Economic justice will come through the organization of economic agencies . . . As the legal mind dominates Congress, it is hard to make a Congressional committee understand that there is no way that Congress can create industrial good will by law.

As against this ineffectuality, Gompers saw the only means to permanent progress in what he termed 'voluntarism' – that is, negotiations pursued between organs such as unions and management free from governmental interference and sanctions. 'I have persistently held that economic organizations ought to be free to operate as economic needs developed.' Law was general, inflexible, and underwrote only the lowest possible gains. Legal minimum wage rates (for example) were liable to become the maximum. Political bargaining and compromising were performed in ignorance of labour's true needs, and might well prevent a particular union from going as far as its economic power could take it. An artificial terminus would thus be set to an economic process otherwise illimitable. Economic advance should not be placed at the mercy of political forces. What government gave, government could take away again; and the workers would thereby be drawn into political action merely in order to secure amendment of what political action had established. Altogether, government was 'simply not competent to conduct industry, to work out the salvation of industry, or to teach industry which paths to walk'.

Furthermore, Gompers professed to see an ethical consideration. Reliance on all but a modicum of governmental action might harm the worker's own initiative and self-reliance. The AFL ought therefore to resist, even in wartime, excessive governmental regulation of industrial affairs:

Doing for people what they can and ought to do for themselves
is a dangerous experiment. In the last analysis the welfare of
the workers depends upon their own initiative.

There is a strange spirit abroad in these times. The whole
people is hugging the delusion that law is a panacea ... What
can be the result of this tendency but the softening of the
moral fibre of the people? ... We must not allow ourselves to
drift upon a policy of excessive regulation by legislation, – a
policy that eats at and will surely undermine the very
foundations of personal liberty. We do not want to place more
power in the hands of the government to investigate and
regulate the lives, the conduct and the freedom of America's
workers.

The attempts of government to establish wages at which
workmen may work is in the experience of history the
beginning of an era, and a long era, of industrial slavery.

A fortiori the AFL should oppose any development of modern
social services. Federal insurance plans, for example, not only
'cannot remove or prevent poverty', but 'there must necessarily
be a weakening of the spirit and virility when compulsory insurance is provided for so large a number of citizens of the
state'. Once again, the consonance of this attitude with the
current individualism of American society generally might
serve to make the new labour movement appear truly indigenous
and respectable. But one also feels at times that Gompers
saw in the state a potentially rival benefactor which might eventually weaken a union's control over its own rank and file.

All these were reasons why craft unionists who were not
socialists should have rated political action rather low. But
they did not neglect it entirely. The half-dozen unions of the
FOTLU, meeting for the first time at Terre Haute in 1881,
framed their legislative objectives in twelve resolutions, and
then laid down the manner of pursuing them in a thirteenth
which urged that 'all trades and labour organizations secure
representation in all law-making bodies by means of the ballot'.
In the following year they made provision for a full-time lobbyist
at Washington. 'I was increasingly conscious,' wrote Gompers,
whose New York cigarmakers had since 1864 kept a representative at Albany throughout sessions of the state legislature,

'that only a full-time Legislative Committee could protect labour's interests.' And although the AFL's headquarters remained at Indianapolis until 1896, Article II of its constitution gave notice of intention 'to secure legislation in the interest of the working masses'. Its president maintained personal contact with occupants of the White House from Hayes onward, and with McKinley's tenure this relationship became a close one. By his own account, Gompers was offered a cabinet post by Bryan on the possibility of the latter's election in 1896, but declined all administrative posts save unsalaried ones, such as a seat on the New York state factory investigation committee of 1912.

As to its relations with Congress, the AFL from 1896 onward maintained a National Legislative Committee in Washington while Congress was sitting, to draft bills, reason with legislators, prepare material for their speeches, and appear at committee hearings. By 1910 it had come close enough to matters of procedure for Gompers to lend a hand in overthrowing Speaker Cannon, whose dictatorial rule had consigned so many liberal proposals to the crematorium of the Judiciary Committee.

Into politics, nevertheless, the AFL would go only so far as was necessary to defend itself or to induce a political climate favourable to that economic organization which was its prime means of self-advancement. Positively, that legislation was desirable which would protect union monopoly in the skilled labour market – restriction of immigration, exclusion of convict-made goods; or which would safeguard conditions of work and categories of worker where these were, if not entirely dependent upon statute law, at least beyond the effective range of economic bargaining – sanitation, occupational disease and hazard, female and child workers, employees of federal, state or municipal government, and seamen. But only for maladies beyond the reach of collective bargaining ought workers to seek political cures. Wages and hours were no proper matter for legislators. The union, not the state, was to be looked to for insurance against unemployment, ill-health or old age. And the unorganizable workers, that is the unskilled, must shift for themselves.

Defensively, the AFL was less concerned to bring government into the labour field than to keep it out. As politicians showed themselves increasingly sensitive to the promptings of business, it behoved the unions concertedly to resist statutory or administrative interference with their freedom to exert economic pressure on the employer. From this arose the AFL's quest for legislation to remove unionism from the scope of the anti-trust law, and to restrict the power of the federal courts in industrial disputes. What brought the Federation to Washington in 1896 was a reinvigorated use of the labour injunction.

The nature of labour's political goals dictated also the method by which it could best pursue them. A movement that accepted the existing order of things, and concerned itself only with immediate and tangible benefits, neither needed nor desired to frame a wide programme of social and economic reconstruction. Any attempt to draft an independent platform, and to enforce it nationally, could bring the labour movement nothing but public dissension and divisions which might spread into the economic field to weaken labour there. The fate of the National Labour Union and the aftermath of the Henry George campaign were awful warnings. Moreover, the existence of a distinct party of labour, by arousing the organized hostility of employers, might recoil upon labour in the all-important process of collective bargaining. And in any case, unless it could beat those two great professional enterprises, the Republican and Democratic parties, at their own game, what was the point of aping their methods? For what would it avail a Labour party to become the refuge for played-out employees of its greater rivals?

Labour, then, if it knew what was good for it, would no more try to form its 'own' party than to coalesce with other groups in a composite 'third party'. Nor ought it to commit its fortunes irrevocably to either one of the historic parties, for to do so would place itself doubly in jeopardy – of being taken for granted when that party was in power and of losing all influence when it was not. Instead the AFL's president held that the way to wrest maximum political concessions was to preserve a posture of 'non-partisanship' towards the two major associations, whereby neither slate could as a matter of course count upon labour's endorsement, which would go in any particular area to the highest bidder. As Gompers put it:

We must be partisan for a principle and not for a party . . .
Labour must learn to use parties to advance our principles,
and not allow political parties to manipulate us for their own
achievement.

Since Democrats and Republicans were *not* principled, they
were always open to bargaining. In return for favourable
legislation, or for immunity from unfavourable, labour would
offer payment in the common coin of votes.

In accordance with this attitude, the Terre Haute conference
of 1881 prohibited any of its members from 'publicly advocating
the claims of any of the political parties', but added that 'this
should not preclude the advocacy to office of a man who is
pledged purely and directly to labour measures'. During the
next four years the conventions of FOTLU and its successor
disavowed any intention of partisanship, the 1895 convention
of the AFL inserting Section 8 into Article III of its constitution:
– 'Party politics, whether they be Democratic, Republican,
Socialistic, Populistic, Prohibitionist or any other, shall have
no place in the conventions of the American Federation of
Labour'. In the following year a resolution was approved that
'no officer of the AFL be allowed to use his official position in
the interests of a political party'; and the 1897 convention
declared for the 'independent use of the ballot by the trade
unionists and workmen united regardless of party, that we may
elect men from our own ranks to make new laws and administer
them along the lines laid down' in the annual conventions, and
'secure the impartial judiciary that will not govern us by
arbitrary injunction of the courts, nor act as the pliant tools of
corporate wealth'.

To 'reward your friends and punish your enemies' – an
adjuration which later passed into popular use – was to demonstrate that the AFL's concern was with measures before parties;
that it would not repeat earlier attempts to initiate a broad
political movement, but would probe the attitudes of major
party candidates towards labour issues. It was Gompers's own
claim to have 'spread the gospel of independent voting' based

upon intelligent understanding of the issues involved in the
election. The labour movement, as I understood it, was

responsible for seeing to it that the wage-earners understood economic issues involved in elections. This has been the basis of the educational work which I have undertaken in different campaigns.

On the strength of this claim his successors have frequently credited him with having introduced labour to 'political education'. But very little money was spent under this head by the AFL when Gompers was master of it. It may be doubted, also, whether 'principled' political activity ran comfortably in harness with opportunist and piecemeal economic. The historian, as he follows labour's fortunes through the ensuing half-century, is more concerned to evaluate Gompersism by its long-term results, to which we must now turn.

The first ten years of the AFL's life appeared largely to validate Gompers's doctrines. Despite a disastrous defeat in the strike of 1894 at Homestead, Pennsylvania, where the most powerful union America had yet seen – the Amalgamated Iron and Steel Workers – were extinguished by the Carnegie Steel Company, the new movement rode out the financial panic of 1893 and the three lean years that followed, to become the first American labour organization to survive a major slump. Thereafter, on the principle that the strike was the way to win, the contract the way to bind, the AFL remained stable enough gradually to extend industrial government by collective bargaining into one industry after another as the pace of economic development quickened. In 1898 was signed the first of a series of national trade agreements, annually reviewable and usually embodying the means of conciliation and arbitration, which spread outwards from the mining, foundry and machine industries to embrace more and more American workers. When in 1897 the Federation moved into the nation's capital city, its ¼m. members represented about 60% of the organized labour force of the USA. By 1903 this proportion had risen to 80%, and thereafter until the 1920s never fell below 74%; and no single intervening year saw a decline of as much as 10% of a membership which by 1914 had crossed the two million mark.

Negatively, too, Gompers's aversion to politics appeared vindicated by governmental action itself. During the 1890s the courts struck down attempt after attempt by Congress and the

states to improve the worker's lot by law. Indeed, some legislation might be charged with latent menace, as the Sherman Act
of 1890 showed. This statute provided that

> every contract, combination in the form of trust or otherwise,
> or conspiracy, in restraint of trade or commerce among the
> several states, or with foreign nations, is hereby declared to be
> illegal. Every person who shall make any such contract or
> engage in any such combination or conspiracy, shall be
> deemed guilty of a misdemeanour.

Although the word 'person' was specifically stated to refer
throughout to corporations and associations, this Act was
applied by the courts, from the Pullman strike of 1894 onward,
so as to resuscitate the old common law doctrine of conspiracy,
under a statute armed threefold with criminal penalties, equity
proceedings by restraining order and injunction, and civil suits
for triple damages. This outcome seemed to justify the AFL
leaders' insistence that labour should keep employers away
from the courts and at the bargaining table, and put no trust in
legislatures or elections.

By the turn of the century, moreover, unionism had to meet a
counter-attack by employers using novel methods. The newly-
formed National Association of Manufacturers not only went
over to the offensive in Congress and state legislatures, but
spearheaded a national open-shop drive on a wide front of
heavy industry. With the NAM, and with other anti-union
forces, Gompers felt it prudent to come to terms, if only to
counteract the rising propaganda which presented unionism as
inimical to public welfare. On the grounds, therefore, that it
'helped to establish the practice of accepting labour unions as
an integral social element', he agreed to serve for a while as
vice-chairman to Mark Hanna in the National Civic Federation
– a body dedicated to preaching the co-operation of labour,
capital and public in defining and upholding certain broad
principles of industrial management.

By 1906, however, the National Civic Federation was
patently declining into an agency for educating employers in
'welfare capitalism'. At the same juncture strong criticism from
within and economic defeats from without were swinging the
AFL back into politics. In March of that year 117 international

presidents and vice-presidents received a summons to Washington to confer with the AFL's executive council. Here was prepared a legislative programme, together with a manifesto commonly referred to as Labour's Bill of Grievances, or Bill of Exceptions. Parts of this programme echoed the Knights of Labour – child labour laws, free schools and textbooks, votes for women and abolition of banking manipulations. But the burden of the complaint concerned trade unionism – government's failure to enforce the eight-hour day in federal employment, to protect labour against the menace of immigration (especially oriental), to prohibit the manufacture and sale of convict-made goods, to enforce restrictions on child labour: above all labour was without protection against the misuse of the federal injunction writ. The manifesto, which was presented to the President and the Congress, ended with a threat:

> Labour now appeals to you, and we trust that it may not be
> in vain. But if perchance you may not heed us, we shall
> appeal to the conscience and support of our fellow citizens.

When both manifesto and programme fell on deaf ears, the AFL leaders determined to bring to the rewarding of friends and punishing of enemies some measure of national co-ordination. They instituted a small but permanent Labour Representation Committee in Washington which published a 'text-book' on political issues, emitted appeals and advice, endorsed federal candidates and raised over $8,000 that year. The major parties were pressed to nominate candidates favourable to labour's demands, chief of which was abolition of the injunction; and AFL units were urged to run an independent ticket wherever these representations were ignored. In 1908, when the AFL executive council officially endorsed Bryan for President, labour's demands upon the parties included recognition of the right to organize, prohibition of labour injunctions in industrial disputes, trial by jury in contempt cases, extension of the eight-hour day to all public work, an employer's liability law, a constitutional amendment granting female suffrage, and the creation of a Department of Labour. The six trade unionists who had been returned to Congress in 1906 had by then increased to seventeen and were meeting regularly as a group.

Not till the first Woodrow Wilson administration, however,

was labour to be gratified with significant gains – a nine-hour day for seamen, an eight-hour day for railroadmen in inter-state commerce (the Adamson Act), and above all the prospect of relief at last from anti-trust prosecution afforded by the Clayton Act of 1914. Jubilation over this statute was the greater because of two recent lawsuits which had badly shaken the AFL. In the first of these, known as the Danbury Hatters case, a hat manufacturer had successfully sued for triple damages on grounds of loss of business resulting from a secondary boy-cott instituted by the AFL on behalf of various of its affiliated unions who were striking the company's plants. The Supreme Court found combination in restraint of interstate commerce of a nature prohibited by the Sherman Act (*Loewe v. Lawlor*, 1908). In the consequent settlement for $234,000 to the com-pany, nearly two hundred union members (many of whom had hitherto known nothing of the affair) lost their savings and had their homes attached for fourteen years. Three years later the Court had gone further to apply the Sherman Act to a case essen-tially of primary boycott, where the AFL had included the aggrieved employer's name in the 'We Don't Patronise' pages of the *American Federationist*, with a consequent sharp falling-off in his sales. A restraining order was issued which enjoined even the Federation's attorney from discussing the case; the blacklist immediately disappeared, and for good; and Gompers himself only escaped serving a prison term on a technicality. 'For seven long years,' he wrote, 'we were either presenting briefs or awaiting court decisions. The litigation was expensive and absorbed money, time and energy that were needed for con-structive work.'

By promising alleviation of these conditions, two sections of the Clayton Act raised labour's spirits:

Section 6 Nothing contained in the anti-trust laws shall be construed to forbid the existence and operation of labour ... organizations ... or to forbid or restrain individual members of such organizations from lawfully carrying out the legitimate objects thereof; nor shall such organizations, or the members thereof, be held or construed to be illegal combinations or conspiracies in restraint of trade, under the anti-trust laws ...

Section 20 No restraining order or injunction shall be
granted by any court of the United States . . . in any case . . .
involving or growing out of a dispute concerning terms or
conditions of employment, . . . or from doing any act or
thing which might lawfully be done in the absence of such
dispute.

Thereby, very sweeping concessions seemed to be granted
American workers – freedom to associate and to use their
traditional weapons without fear of crippling injunctions or
prosecutions under anti-trust law. No wonder Gompers hailed
the Act as 'labour's Magna Charta'.

The first Wilson administration also established a truly
independent Department of Labour, thus ending half a century
of agitation. In 1884 Congress had created a Bureau of Labour
Statistics within the Department of the Interior, four years later
had raised it to an independent section, and in 1903 placed the
head of a duple Department of Commerce and Labour within
the President's cabinet. The new Department of Labour
separated off in March 1913 embodied the Bureau of Immigration and Naturalization, a Children's Bureau, and a Division
of Conciliation whose itinerant corps of professionals were to do
notably good work in industrial pacification everywhere outside the railroads. The first Secretary of Labour, the Scottish-
born William B. Wilson, was formerly secretary-treasurer of
the United Mine Workers and chairman of the House Committee of Labour: and for the next forty years, till Eisenhower's
presidency, all his successors save two were trade unionists of
some sort.

When to these innovations are added statutes governing
industrial safety, workmen's compensation, apprenticeship and
vocational education, and the minimum wage, the first Wilson
administration may appear in retrospect to have contained the
genesis of modern social security and labour welfare in the USA.
Bearing in mind, too, parallel or complementary legislation in
many of the states, 'by 1917', an AFL official could justly claim,
'practically every demand set out in the Bill of Grievances had
been enacted into law'. But it is questionable how much credit
his own organization deserved. The AFL's first electoral campaign of 1906 had amounted to little more than a few local

engagements in which no Congressional candidate marked down had been defeated. The Federation had made no attempt to activate opinion outside its own ranks, and not even its own top officers had unanimously gone along with the official endorsement of 1908. Further, the significance of the Clayton Act, for whose passage the Federation claimed major credit, soon dwindled under judicial interpretation; while the enactment of the Adamson bill was directly due to Wilson's personal intervention under pressure of the railroad Brotherhoods' threat to call a nationwide strike. For other liberal measures ripening in the genial climate of this period the American people were more indebted to the imaginative leadership provided by such bodies as the American Association for Legislation and the National Consumers' League, led by the 'intellectuals' and Socialists whom Gompers held in such disdain. How little overall the labour movement, or any other, had yet succeeded in changing the tenor of American capitalism was revealed by the US Commission on Industrial Relations, whose final report of 1915, with its account of concentration of industrial ownership and control under leaders implacably hostile to unionism, made comfortless reading. Any general transformation of Labour's position within the system must await the impact of external forces.

This impact the First World War provided. From the end of 1914 the expansion of defence industries, the abrupt drop in immigration, and later the conscribing of over 5m. of the nation's fittest young men, led to a manpower shortage and keen competition for labour in American industry. The defence boom indeed brought such wide profit margins that employers preferred to concede wage increases rather than risk stoppage of so lucrative a productivity: their willingness was enhanced by the government's acceptance, with entry into the war, of the principle of the 'cost plus' contract. When in December 1917 the federal government moved farther into the industrial scene by taking over rail and water transport and certain key industries, it brought with it enlightened labour policies – collective bargaining, really effective machinery of arbitration and improved working rules – and more generally fostered the unionism upon whose self-government it must greatly rely for such desiderata as wage stability and minimal turnover of employment. Like business, with whom it observed a temporary truce, American unionism was respited when anti-trust legislation was placed in abeyance for the duration. With management, too, it met in a bipartite War Committee on Labour.

The prevailing pattern, however, was tripartite. On the huge and supreme Council of National Defence representatives of labour, capital and government met to draw up general principles of wartime labour policy, including most of the demands made by assembled union leaders in March 1917, on the brink of America's involvement in world conflict. Essentially these demands were that organized labour (meaning principally the AFL) be recognized as spokesman for all wage-earners, including 'those who have not yet organized', and that it be represented on all wartime governmental agencies concerned with labour matters. Of many such agencies the most powerful was the War Labour Administration, set up in January 1918 with the Secretary of Labour at its head. For the rest of that year the United States knew its closest approximation to British wartime regulation.

The WLA was successor to a War Labour Conference Board, whose plenary jurisdiction over all fields of defence production had done much to encourage collective bargaining and raise work standards. According to its succinct statement of policy, 'the right of workers to organize in trade unions and to bargain collectively, through chosen representatives, shall not be denied, abridged or interfered with by the employers in any manner whatsoever': on the other hand 'the workers, in the exercise of their right to organize, shall not use coercive measures of any kind to induce employers to bargain or deal therewith'. Strikes and lockouts were outlawed. Employers were forbidden to discharge hands for membership of a union. Union shops were to remain unionized but the existence of a non-union shop was not to be considered a grievance if the means of collective bargaining were provided. The basic eight-hour day was to apply in all cases where existing law required it, and in others was to be settled by mutual agreement having regard to the workers' safety and health. All workers were entitled to a living wage, which should be equal for both sexes. This code extended to nearly all industries the principles adopted for a few by a Presidential Mediation Commission, and an employer unwilling to subscribe to them would appear something less than a patriot. In return labour forewent only the precarious right to strike: truly, it possessed little else to concede.

To apply and clarify this code was the task of a National War Labour Board, which bore also the responsibility to mediate and conciliate in industrial disputes threatening war production. In addition, a much-criticized War Labour Policies Board sought to control labour supply, reduce competitive bidding for workers, and stabilize employment conditions by standardizing wages. More durably, within the Labour Department itself was created the United States Employment Service, of eventual peacetime benefit. This intimacy between unionism and government was symbolized when President Wilson, dedicating the AFL's new Washington headquarters on Massachusetts Avenue, declared that in future no successor to his office would be able to ignore organized labour. Of greater practical benefit was the experience accruing to union leaders who for the emergency worked in harness with national administrators, and especially to the corps of AFL officials in contact with the President, the Cabinet and government departments at the centre of operations.

This satisfying liaison did not long outlive the armistice of November 1918. By then Wilson was physically and politically ailing, and the Democrats were in a minority in both houses of Congress. With the generally desired 'return to normalcy' many federal agencies of concern to labour were discarded or reduced. True, the federal government did not evacuate the economic field without some attempt to place the post-war labour-management relationship upon a stable footing. In October 1919 Wilson convened a tripartite National Industrial Conference 'to discover such methods as had not already been tried out of bringing labour and capital into close co-operation'. But when after eleven fruitless days it foundered upon the rocky principle of collective bargaining, and could not be refloated, the two sides were left to work out their own solutions face to face.

Disappointed at the withdrawal of government, and apprehensive about the intentions of business, American workers resorted to economic pressure of the most direct kind. Management for its part was impatient to resume its pre-war relationship with labour and to 'shake down' a too bumptious unionism. And so the brief post-armistice recession, unguided from

Washington, saw a sharp increase in the number and acerbity of labour disturbances, the year 1919 establishing a new record for the number of wage earners involved in them – over 4m. strikers in nearly 4,000 stoppages. On 8 January 1920 a strike more than fifteen weeks old ended when 300,000 steelworkers sustained the biggest defeat American unionism had yet known. Disasters of varying magnitude befell a lockout of the Clothing Workers, a three-month strike of Textile Workers at Lawrence, Mass., a great railway shop strike, and a stay-out of 450,000 coalminers over the winter of 1921–2. The period of industrial contraction which saw the 'battle' of Logan County, West Virginia, the Herrin 'massacres' in Illinois, the five-day strike in Seattle and the police strike in Boston, saw also a diminution of union numbers almost as spectacular as their wartime rise. In five beneficent years trade union membership had doubled itself to stand in 1920 at the peak figure of over 5m. (of whom the AFL claimed more than four-fifths) – a greater increase than for the whole of the period 1897–1914. Early in 1920 wage-cutting became general, and within less than three years more than $1\frac{1}{2}$ m. members had melted away.

Strife and calamity on this scale may lead one to overlook such positive proposals as labour actually made. A special committee of AFL elders drafted, and its national convention of 1919 endorsed, a 'reconstruction programme', some of whose demands went beyond those of 1906 – the 44-hour week, tax reform, a national housing programme, and public regulation of mines and certain utilities. Under pressure from the Railroad Brotherhoods, and over Gompers's protests, it indeed subsequently endorsed the so-called Plumb Plan to nationalize the railroads. But after Congress had rejected this, it did not press the matter. If America were on the brink of a new social order, the old union hierarchy were not deeply concerned to shape it. 'Wait in patience and fortitude,' was Gompers's advice, 'until the day when the nation has spoken the last word.'

Such counsel, and the old 'economism' from which it sprang, were by now dissatisfying to a growing fraction of his organization's own membership. Discontent was signalled when in 1921 the United Mineworkers' convention called upon the national executive for aggressive electoral intervention on an independent basis; and it was by the candidature (labelled 'progressive')

4

of a senior UMW official, John L. Lewis, that in the same year Gompers's re-election to the AFL presidency was for the first time since 1894 seriously threatened. In 1924, when the Democratic nominee for President was a conservative corporation lawyer, Gompers from his deathbed conceded that his executive council must *faute de mieux* endorse La Follette. Even so, their endorsement was coupled with the caveat that 'the co-operation hereby urged is not a pledge of identification with an independent party movement, or a third party'. And when La Follette failed, the AFL's mite of patronage was withdrawn.

As for its machinery for political intervention, the only modifications the AFL made at this period were small. For the 1920 Presidential campaign, when it supported Cox, the three-man Labour Representation Committee of 1906 was expanded to include the entire executive council and heads of all the trade departments, renamed the National Non-Partisan Political Campaign Committee, and, instead of being re-formed for each campaign season, made part of the establishment. A beginning was attempted, though not systematically maintained, of compiling the voting records of Congressional candidates. A fund-raising drive in the same year brought $53,934 into the Committee's coffers: but after 1924 the collection of money on a national scale was abandoned, though some affiliated unions continued to make their own arrangements. A corresponding permanency was given lobbying arrangements when on 26 May 1921 all legislative agents of AFL internationals and departments, thirty or forty strong, combined in a Conference Committee of Trade Union Legislative Representatives. Here, in company with representatives of the Railroad Brotherhoods, pending legislation was analysed, differences of opinion reconciled, and joint resources marshalled. It is disappointing to record that, if we except statutory restriction of immigration, the only appreciable gain made by labour in Washington between 1918 and 1932 was the Railway Labour Act of 1926.

More significantly, these small political gains were outweighed by serious and frustrating setbacks. Not only was more labour legislation held unconstitutional in the 1920s than in any other decade of American history. A 'strict constructionist' Supreme Court, holding each case to be determined 'on its own circumstances', dashed unionism's hopes for a more liberal interpretation of existing statutes. Consequently, the number of injunctions issued, and of damage and contempt cases preferred, against unions or their leaders in the post-war decade was on yearly average greater than in any comparable period before 1914. Within three years of passage of the Clayton Act, for example, the Court granted an injunction against the United Mine Workers in the course of upholding a yellow-dog contract on behalf of coal operators determined to keep unions out of West Virginia and eastern Kentucky (*Hitchman Coal & Coke Co. v. Mitchell*, 1917). Five years later the same union suffered an even heavier reverse when the Court upheld the award by an inferior court of $200,000 damages (tripled under the Sherman Act) against an Arkansas local which had violently resisted the attempt of a coal company to revert, by wholesale methods, from unionized to non-unionized labour. While absolving from responsibility in this particular case the union's national organization, and allowing that the action of its local had not amounted to interference with inter-state commerce, the Court nevertheless made a general ruling that a labour union though unincorporated was a legal entity suable in its own name, and its funds subject to execution in suits for torts committed in the course of a strike (*United Mine Workers v. Coronado Coal Co.*, 1922). These two cases alone furnished the employers' open-shop drive of the 1920s with an unassailable legal bastion which a debilitated unionism could neither sap nor storm.

At the same time unionism itself continued to be judicially inhibited from deploying even those siege and battery weapons whose use the Clayton Act, on any straightforward reading, expressly said might not be enjoined at all. Thus in 1921, in the case of a Machinists' local striking a low-wage, non-unionized manufactory of printing presses, and bringing pressure on customers not to buy its products, a majority of the Supreme Court held that it had not been Congress's intention in 1914 to legalize the secondary boycott at all (*Duplex Printing Press Co. v. Deering*). A few years later a local of the Stone Cutters struck to enforce a provision of its constitution prohibiting members from handling stone cut by non-union men. On appeal the Supreme Court, while agreeing that the strike had as its sole and lawful end the organization of the plaintiff's employees, nevertheless

ruled that the union had in pursuit of that end employed unlawful means, to wit, the restriction of inter-state commerce by
taking away the petitioners' customers (*Bedford Cut Stone Co.
v. Journeymen Stone Cutters' Association*, 1927). As to picketing,
the same Court in 1921 drastically restricted the bounds of per-
missibility when it held that the posting of more than one 'mis-
sionary' – whose activities were closely circumscribed – at
each gate constituted intimidation. When in 1925 a federal
circuit court ruled picketing to be illegal in the absence of a
strike, the local concerned did not deem worthwhile the expense
of carrying the case further. The most sweeping instance of the
new 'government by injunction' was probably a case of 1922,
where the Department of Justice in order to end the railroad
shop strike secured from a federal court an order restraining all
union activities down to conversation between strikers, and
applicable not to them alone but to 'all of their attorneys,
servants, agents, associates, members and employers and all
persons acting in aid or conjunction with them'.

Sometimes the Court appeared to be saying that the act of
1914 had merely codified, without at all modifying, the best
practices of pre-existing law; at other times even to be intimat-
ing that the right to issue injunctions was an inherent power of
the courts not subject to legislative abridgement. In two minor
respects only did the Clayton Act in these years lighten labour's
lot – by providing for jury trial in cases of indirect contempt
(i.e. where the contempt complained of was also in violation of
a statute), and by fixing a limit upon the imposable penalty. But
these small gains were more than offset by an ironically unfore-
seen consequence of the Act. To the three sanctions of the
Sherman Act (criminal prosecutions, suits for damages, and
governmental injunctions) was now added the private injunction
suit, and thereby a new facility offered the employer as direct
mover of the machinery of justice.

To the employer we must now return. Under one principle
of the War Labour Conference Board he could not be compelled to recognize union representatives or spokesmen other
than from among his own employees; and many wartime employers had therefore encouraged within their plants, not genuine
collective bargaining, but the erection of 'employers' works
councils' and 'employee representation plans'. Upon this

foundation, and guided by the NAM's Committee on Readjustment After the War, peacetime management proceeded to build. In 1921 open-shop organizations in every state came together in the 'American Plan'. Associations of manufacturers, boards of trade, chambers of commerce, bankers, builders and even farmers united in extending direct aid to their membership with money, spies, strikebreakers and blacklists of union agitators. Once again the public sympathy aroused by such slogans as 'free shops for free men' was canalized into 'citizens' associations'. As a consequence, while unionism proper declined, company unionism doubled between 1922 and 1928 until in the latter year it covered $1\frac{1}{2}$ m. workers.

Other legacies of war proved equally adaptable by management in peace. Government's preoccupation with industrial manpower, for instance, had fostered the techniques of Frederic W. Taylor and others. The new 'scientific management' appeared to offer reasonable and objective standards of efficiency in place of crude bargaining, while 'personnel management' promised to make the employer's supervisory function seem less arbitrary and even perfectly disinterested. Another wartime novelty had been the reference of matters affecting productivity to semi-permanent agencies of joint consultation. Characteristic of the 'welfare capitalism' of the 1920s was the blossoming of numerous employer-controlled plans for workers' pensions and life insurance. Employee stock ownership, too, was encouraged and sometimes even mandatory. A National Industrial Conference Board of 1928 estimated that in that year over a million workers had subscribed for over a billion dollars' worth of securities of the companies who employed them. Positing as it did a 'mutuality of interest' between labour and management in preserving and heightening the vitality and rewards of the capitalist system as it stood, what resistance to these new trends could the 'business unionism' of Gompers offer which would not seem blind unreason? Add to this the phenomenal growth under the Republicans between 1921 and 1929 of the nation's prosperity and productivity, appealing confidently to the imagination of every citizen, and the triumph of capitalism appeared not only economic and political, but spiritual also.

In fact, however, the most impressive technological expansion occurred in areas where unionism was non-existent, and whither the AFL, continuing to ignore the unskilled and semi-skilled, had no mind to follow. In metal, leather, rubber, petroleum and chemical industries, in communications and public utilities, unions either did not exist or were confined to the tiny minority of the skilled. Places like Detroit and Los Angeles were virtually open-shop cities. 'Gompersism' had pinned its hopes mainly to the exploitation of economic methods. So long as it controlled the most significant sections of the country's work-force, that was a reasonable risk. The odds became less favourable as the relative size and importance of the skilled crafts diminished. Yet the AFL conventions of 1919 and 1921 voted down well-reasoned proposals for the assimilation of industrial workers. The consequence became plain when, the immediate post-war recession behind it, the Federation not only failed to pick up but in each year of industrial expansion (save 1927) relatively declined. By 1930 the proportion of organized workers in the USA had dropped to about 10% of the total non-agricultural labour force (as compared with 19·4% in 1920). Allowing as these figures do for a growth in the number of potentially organizable workers, this was a retreat almost to the pre-war position of 1910. Moreover this organized 10% was split between more than 120 unions, either of the small craft type or in stagnant or declining areas of the economy such as railroads and coalmines; and even here losses had been heavy. Building trades workers, the most conservative element, now constituted one-third of the AFL's membership.

The 1920s, therefore, stand out as a period of increasingly disparate wealth, when real wages of many employees increased but in no sense proportionately to profits and dividends. In the last year of the Hoover administration the 200 largest non-banking corporations of the United States had combined assets of $81b., or nearly half the corporate wealth of the country. In the same year nearly 6m. American families had collective annual incomes of less than $1,000 apiece. Industry throve while unionism declined. Here was a quite unprecedented phenomenon, and one fundamentally at odds with the Gompersian thesis. Business unionism in the boom era was failing to bring home the bacon. 'Voluntarism' now meant that what most workers were getting was only what industry voluntarily conceded. Side by side with the boom went the stretch-out system, the sweat-shop, child labour and a widespread flouting of factory laws. In 'a billion-dollar country', as Senator Reed called it, large sections of a non-unionized steel industry were working a twelve-hour day, seven-day week. If the year 1929 saw an all-time low in strike figures, this was not because the union larder was full, but because an ageing and demoralized leadership which feared disputes as a source of further fragmentation did all they could to suppress economic militarism, themselves providing strikebreakers on occasion. Upon this wasted and decaying body 'hold-up' unionists and racketeers battened as never before. Such were the signs when President Hoover in his inaugural address of 4 March 1929 proclaimed to the world that the problem of poverty had been solved.

What debilitated the old unionism in America (it is important to stress the point) was not the Great Depression but the decade of prosperity preceding it. Of the Depression itself the many sagas need no retelling here. Suffice it to say that one year after the great stock market crash of 23 October 1929 and the precipitous downswing of the whole business cycle, those Americans officially registered as without full-time employment totalled over 7m. The true number of workless during the winter of 1932–3 – the winter of closing banks and scrip currency, of search for a steady dime an hour and interminable breadlines; the winter when even over Pittsburgh the skies were clear – can never be known. Twelve million is a popular guess. But what signified was that organized labour was even less competent to succour them than were the radicals it had rejected. The British general election of 1923 had seen 191 members of the party of Labour returned to Westminster: six years later it had become the strongest section there. In the USA a labour movement tied to the old, almost apolitical 'economism' stood helplessly by while starving strikers were herded off the streets, arrested and beaten up by corporation or state police, without even minimal guidance in self-defence. Therein lies the plainest indictment of a labour movement which in the twentieth century put its main trust in purely economic methods of self-advancement.

For in its darkest hour the movement Gompers had led could find no answer in his philosophy. It had set out by proclaiming for all American workers 'the right to be full sharers in the abundance which is the product of their brain and brawn, and in the civilization of which they are the founders and mainstay'. When private capitalism collapsed, it could not secure the majority of them a competence. For the first quarter-century of its life, the AFL's programme had been congruent enough with its milieu. But after the brief spell of governmental favour under the duress of world war it had settled back into its old paths, on a relatively even narrower basis which ignored the new industries. It had once prided itself upon its opportunism: but it had long ceased to be able to recognize its opportunities. When the old order which it posited spectacularly failed, only a revivified government could rescue the nation. Thenceforward, as labour was to learn in the 1930s, political engagement could no longer be regarded as the instrument of last resort.

3

The new government of
Franklin Roosevelt

The vote – 57·4% of the popular poll – which in 1932 carried
the Presidency and every state but five for the Democrats,
which brought their total of governorships to 40, and which
swept them into the House in sufficient number to outweigh
their opponents by nearly three to one, was an anti-Republican
rather than a pro-Democrat vote. It was hard to see what else
it could have been. The electorate had not been offered any
novel social philosophy. The Democratic platform had mentioned organized labour only once, in a vague notice of intention
to revise the anti-trust laws 'for the better protection of labour
and the small producer and distributor'; and if it advocated
'continuous responsibility of government for human welfare',
this was no more than what circumstances had already compelled the outgoing Administration to acknowledge. The victorious party's only specific promise, in fact, had been to cut
federal spending by about 25%.

It was through their new leader then, if at all, that liberal
ideas must have access to political power. But Roosevelt's
attitude to reform was scarcely better known than his party's.
Even when, after two years of office, he spoke in January
1935 to Congress of 'a new economic order rising out of the
disintegration of the old', the President had no general blueprint, no wide schemes for governmental ownership or radical
redistribution of the national income. For the disintegration

of the old had left not a single part of American society firm enough to serve as a nucleus for reconstruction. The call to government for remedial action was in 1932 a cry raised by the entire nation and not, as in earlier American radical movements, by one or two discontented groups only. A vague theory of universal co-operation was therefore the reformer's best point of departure. Because the Depression had been a national and not merely a labour crisis, so the New Deal, if it were a revolution at all, was certainly not a labour revolution merely, but a national revolution of which labour unions were among the principal beneficiaries. If it inherited some of the goals of American radicalism, it bore scant trace of the ethico-religious character of earlier 'progressive' movements. And anything about it that smacked of revolution may be explained by contrasting Roosevelt's dramatic words and actions with the cautious manipulations of his predecessor. For himself, he preferred to present the New Dealer as 'the true conservative'.

Still less was the New Deal beholden to any ideology. At a speed which kept his Administration not too far ahead of public opinion the President moved towards pragmatic goals, such as would put more money in the pocket of the American citizen, and throughout the course saw his task as being not only to formulate public policy but to plan the institutional strategy necessary to its enactment. This technical aspect of his job, it seems, pleased him as much as any. The result was a mingling of the expedient and the principled, the improvisatory and the permanent, traceable to no one theory or theorist of government in particular, where purposes of relief and recovery are not easily disentangled from those of long-term reform.

In one field, however, improvisation was pure and unalloyed. By January 1933 the cautious provision for public works which Congress had made two years earlier had long since been overtaken by events. While recognizing some responsibility for the health of the national economy, Hoover's attempts to discharge it had been limited by his view that 'the whole function of government is to bring about a condition of affairs favourable to the beneficial development of private enterprise'. The steps which he had taken in January 1932 were based on the principle that the chief, if not the sole, method requisite for reviving employment was direct governmental aid to business –

the policy described by his critics as one of trickle and drip or, more coarsely, of feeding the sparrows by feeding the horses. In May, and with an election imminent, his Administration at last grasped the nettle of direct public relief. The functions of the Reconstruction Finance Corporation, originally erected to subsidize distressed banks, railroad and insurance companies, were extended to include the making of emergency loans to states and municipalities to the tune of $200m. at 3% interest. Although the federal government's role was confined to book-keeping, the act did provide a nuclear regional organization which Hoover's successor took over.

The newcomer, having first eased the pressure of competition upon the older unemployed by providing work for their juniors through the Civilian Conservation Corps, in May 1933 created the Federal Emergency Relief Administration under Harry Hopkins, who is reported to have disbursed more than $5m. in relief during his first two hours in office. After twelve months the FERA had laid out $1½b. in a vast programme which handled 17m. cases. But 'our greatest primary task', Roosevelt had said in his first inaugural address, 'is to put the people to work'. In the following autumn Congress passed the National Industrial Recovery Act, one part of which provided for an extensive public works programme supported by an initial appropriation of $3,300m. A Public Works Administration, under Harold Ickes, was to give financial help in promoting socially useful public projects, and to make loans to private employers for constructional purposes, with power to scrutinize all contracts entered into by non-governmental bodies. Until the PWA could absorb them, some 4m. people were to be carried through the winter on the books of a Civil Works Administration, where Hopkins was in charge of a decentralized programme (set up in a single week) of purely short-term projects, of doubtful social utility but greatly preferable to breadlines, grocery tickets and the means test. By January 1935 about 5½m. work relief cases had been handled, involving over twenty million citizens. In April Congress conflated all emergency relief agencies – some sixty of them – into a single $5b. programme whereunder Hopkins headed the biggest New Deal employing and spending agency, the Works Progress Administration. Though the WPA underwent a mounting barrage of criticism, yet during each of the fiscal years 1934, –5 and –6, Congress continued to vote between $8m. and $9m. for relief and public works, and more than 20m. Americans continued to be directly dependent on them. At the same time the government brought back machinery for coping with unemployment at normal levels, which since 1917 had been allowed to rust. In June 1933 the United States Employment Service, whose resuscitation Hoover had vetoed, was restored by Congress and set to co-ordinate a national network of employment offices and to subsidize state bodies of this kind.

The case of unemployment relief illustrates Rooseveltian policies at their most improvisatory. Yet it is as clear an example as any of the new and peculiarly direct concern of government for the welfare and security of its citizens. This concern was mirrored in many facets of policy. Fiscally, men saw it reflected in the concept of 'social' investment to correct deficiencies in private investment; in the preoccupation of economic analysts with national budgetary aggregates rather than with internal price manipulation; in the 'wealth tax' and the attack on monopoly practices; and in a doubling of the percentage of national income derived from federal taxation, made possible by the development of new sources to tap. But it is by its beneficence to one class of citizen in particular that the New Deal marks a watershed in the history of American labour. In three capacities the worker found himself a peculiar beneficiary of the new order; – as a member of that 'one third of a nation ill-housed, ill-clad, ill-nourished'; as a wage-earner of low pur-chasing power; and as a trade union member possessing un-equal bargaining strength *vis-à-vis* management. We may conveniently consider him as filling each of these roles in turn.

In the first capacity, as a member of an economically de-pressed class, the American industrial worker benefited like other citizens from the government's recognition of the need to preserve capitalism by hedging it round in the interests of the artisan, the farmer, the small land owner and the small in-vestor. Calling for 'social justice through social action', Roose-velt proposed to Congress three types of security. One he des-cribed as 'security of a livelihood through the better use of the national resources of the land we live in': its most monumental instrument was to be the Tennessee Valley Authority. The others were 'security against the major hazards and vicissitudes of life', and 'the security of decent homes'.

The field of social security was minutely surveyed by a special committee, whose report provided the basis for a Social Security Act to alleviate the worst privations of the jobless, the aged and the dependent. Its provisions for unemployment insurance, in contrast with the British Act of 1911, introduced not a national scheme but a joint enterprise where the federal government used its taxing power to stimulate the states into making limited grants for limited periods to their involuntarily workless. Fear of constitutional challenge necessitated a method – a general payroll tax upon the employer – somewhat cumbersome, yet so successful that within two years all states had enacted unemployment compensation laws satisfying the conditions laid down by the federal administrative authority, a three-man Social Security Board.

For the aged the Act established, first, a purely federal scheme under which employers and employees in certain occupational categories would pay annually a rising percentage (beginning at 1%) of wages paid or received into a retirement reserve fund from which eligible workers and their wives might benefit on reaching the age of sixty-five. By an amendment of 1939 these benefits were extended to include pensions for beneficiaries' widows and dependent children, and the scheme was then renamed Old Age and Survivors Insurance. Secondly, at sixty-five a citizen might be eligible in one of three categories of special need to receive assistance under a scheme operated jointly by the federal and state governments: the federal government would pay matching grants of up to $15 per person towards the cost of state schemes where these met the Board's specifications. Within three years every state had qualified for this assistance, and within ten years the names of nearly 65m. people had been entered upon the federal insurance rolls. Federal aid was also forthcoming for vocational rehabilitation and for maintaining and expanding state and local health services.

In seeking to provide its citizens with 'the security of decent homes' the new Administration was faced with a housing market so depressed by lack of cheap financing that long-term mortgages were practically unprocurable and interest on short-term private loans ran as high as 10%. To buy up distress mortgages the government immediately created the Home Owners' Loan Corporation, which probably saved a million families from dispossession, and by an Act of 1934 set up a Federal Housing Administration which underwrote loans made by private lenders to the tune (after eighteen years) of $31b. But merely to insure private builders did not immediately benefit low income families to the extent desired. In 1937 direct federal help was therefore given to local public authorities in planning, building and maintaining their own low-rent housing projects according to their own determination of needs. Within ten years nearly three-quarters of the states were co-operating and new homes had been constructed for 168,000 families in 262 communities.

For relief of the citizen in his second and third aspects, as a wage earner and as a trade unionist, the Roosevelt Administration proposed one sovereign specific – expand the volume of employment by expanding purchasing power. Labour was seen as having on the one hand an inadequate share of the national income, on the other unequal bargaining power with employers. The new policy endeavoured to correct both these deficiencies: the former directly by wage and hour legislation, the latter indirectly by helping workers to help themselves through an extension of that process of organizing which alone could improve their bargaining position. Statute law was to be the instrumentality, firstly for laying down a floor of minimal standards, and secondly for removing impediments to collective bargaining and so enabling the workers further to raise those standards above the statutory minimum. The first Rooseveltian statute directly to affect organized labour, the National Industrial Recovery Act of 1933, was a characteristically New Deal measure in that (besides relief) its express intent was to increase consumption by increasing purchasing power, and in that it aimed to do so partly by wage regulation and partly by fostering the growth of trade unionism.

The matter of the volume of employment, however, was not a simple one. The preceding Administration had correctly diagnosed the national malaise as one of over-production and over-capitalization. The co-operation of industry had therefore been sought, and all too briefly obtained, for a measure of planned

industrial and agricultural restriction. In proposing to extend
to all industries Hoover's policy of self-restraint, his Democratic successor was determined to have governmental supervision of the process and, by direct pressure if necessary, to
secure business's co-operation. But experience taught that this
co-operation must be voluntary in form. Too great a degree of
compulsion might be felt as 'undemocratic' even by unionism,
which was not yet prepared for considerable governmental intervention. And the attitude of the courts was unknown.

Upon goodwill, therefore, the National Recovery Act depended for its efficacy. This spectacular omnibus measure,
which Roosevelt called 'the most important and far-reaching
legislation ever enacted by the American Congress', was an
ambitious attempt to exert indirect federal control over the
entire industrial structure of the country. All participants in
industry were urged to introduce 'self-government' by coming
together to make agreements which would then be incorporated
for each industry in a published code of 'fair competition' that
workers and employers would agree to observe. These codes
were to contain provisions for the regulation of trade practices
and labour standards, the latter to include minimum wages,
maximum hours and the banning of child labour. In return for
a temporary suspension of the anti-trust laws, employers (it was
hoped) would recognize the right of labour to enjoy fair standards and conditions, and to organize. Competition and output would be regulated and the price system re-articulated
without inflation. In all, 731 such codes were drawn up, receiv-
ing the force of law with the President's signature, and industries governed by these instruments saw a rise of over 2m. employed. Minimum wages were set and linked to a basic 35–40
hour week. About 150,000 children under sixteen disappeared
from industry and so did putting-out. A 'little NRA' of this
kind was the salvation of the coal industry.

Putting a floor under wages generally presented the government with fewer administrative or constitutional problems, for
legislative precedent already existed for certain types of work
paid for out of federal funds. In June 1936 Congress passed the
Public Contracts (Walsh-Healey) Act, an elaborate and important measure specifying minimum working conditions – an
8-hour day and a 40-hour week – on all federal works of a

greater value than $10,000. Inflation was to bring many more cases into that category. It may be noted, too, that the federal government's influence was not only direct as the nation's largest employer, but indirect inasmuch as a private employer cannot in practice maintain different wages and conditions as between those of his workers employed on government contracts and those on private. Under Walsh-Healey, wage rates were to be fixed in respective areas after public hearings; certain safety and health standards were laid down; and the employment of children under sixteen years was forbidden. Also significant in this connection were the provisions for workmen's compensation which the great majority of American states were bringing in at the same time.

But the climax of the New Deal's concern for the worker as wage-earner was reached in 1938 with legislation covering (certain categories excepted) all employees in and all goods manufactured for interstate commerce. The Fair Labour Standards Act, like the NRA an omnibus measure, provided for a minimum hourly wage of 25c., whose rate of advance to 40c. an hour would be controlled over seven years by a Wage and Hour Administrator upon the advice of a committee where employers and employed in each particular industry were equally represented. The basic work week was in most industries to be reduced to 40 hours within three years: a work-day longer than the statutory maximum was not prohibited but made more costly. Finally, employment in industries manufacturing for interstate commerce of children under sixteen (under eighteen in the case of hazardous occupations) was at last made effectual.

Much of organized labour was dissatisfied by the caution with which the still low wage minima were approached, and by the exclusion from coverage of the great majority of employees in the retail trade, in domestic service and in agriculture, which thus reduced the statute's operational range from 11m. citizens to fewer than 4m. Nevertheless a most important step forward had been taken when Congress accepted the principle that a minimum standard of life for the worker should be delimited and upheld by law; and the Supreme Court in upholding it recognized Congress's power to regulate directly the terms of industrial employment. While, as with the NRA, full benefit of the Act could only be secured by a strong collective bargaining unit, legal enforcement had superseded the reliance on voluntary co-operation premised by the earlier statute. Unions, moreover, have found a legal charge of statutory violation against an employer to be a valuable publicity move in their campaigns to organize lower-paid workers.

The worker in his third capacity – as a member or potential member of a trade union – had already, before the New Deal began, received some recent help of a negative kind from a law which, though it did not purport directly to promote the right of collective bargaining, declared the employee to be entitled to 'full freedom of association, self-organization, and designation of representatives of his own choosing to negotiate the terms and conditions of his employment . . . free from the interference, restraint, or coercion of employers'. Pressed upon the Administration by the Seventy-Second Congress, the Norris-La Guardia Act of 1932 owed nothing to Hoover, who signed it with reluctance, nor to the AFL, who regarded it with a paralysed scepticism. Its underlying purpose as subsequently interpreted by the Supreme Court (in *U.S. v. Hutcheson* (1940), reversing The *Duplex* and *Bedford Stone* decisions mentioned at pp. 45–6 above) was to restore the broad purpose which Congress thought it had formulated in the Clayton Act but which was frustrated, so Congress believed, by unduly restrictive judicial construction. Its tenor was to widen considerably the concept of the labourer's legitimate interest, and correspondingly the area in which he might be allowed to help himself through organizational activities, by recognizing in those activities a species of property right which must be balanced against the rights and interests of the employer and the public whenever a restraining order was to seek. Unions in pursuit of their collective ends were to be allowed the same freedom from legal intervention that business had always enjoyed.

First, the yellow dog contract, though not absolutely invalidated, was declared 'contrary to the public policy of the United States' and void. Second, the power of these courts to grant an injunction order on a labour dispute (a term herein widely defined) was very sharply restricted. For the actions listed in the Act as non-enjoinable included joining a union, striking, administering strike benefits, peaceful picketing or assembly or any other non-violent method of publicizing the

5

existence of a dispute. Further, the enjoined party was protected against delays in the review of a restraining order, was granted the right to jury trial in cases of contempt, which might now be heard before a judge other than he who issued the injunction. At one stroke Congress cut through the fictions which had frustrated the attempts of American workers to realize their normal aspirations through collective action, and the change was remarkable. Although Norris-La Guardia applied only to federal courts, these had been the most prodigal with injunctions in the past. It remains to add that by 1942 half the states had put similar legislation on their books, and that from the Supreme Court's validation of the Act in 1937 to the passage of the Taft-Hartley Act ten years later, no major employer in the United States succeeded in continuing operations during a strike.

Positive encouragement of collective bargaining, however, attended promulgation of the National Recovery Act, which in the momentous phrases of its Section 7A proclaimed for the first time in American history that

1 Employees shall have the right to organize and to bargain collectively through representatives of their own choosing, and shall be free from interference, restraint or coercion of employers of labour, or of their agents, in the designation of such representatives or in self-organization or in other concerted activities for the purpose of collective bargaining or other mutual aid or protection.
2 No employee and no one seeking employment shall be required as a condition of employment to join any company union or to refrain from joining organizing or assisting a labour organization of his own choosing.

Section 8 then went on to enumerate certain 'unfair labour practices' of the employer, including interference with these rights and refusal to bargain collectively with his employees' representatives as certified by a National Labour Board appointed by the President.

The duties of this agency were to settle, by mediation and voluntary arbitration, disputes arising out of the relevant parts of the Act, and thus clothe its bare terms with administrative interpretation. In less than a year the Board had handled cases

affecting nearly 2m. workers, until in June 1934 it was superseded by a National Labour Relations Board of three full-time
officers with power to subpoena witnesses, hold elections to
determine employees' representatives, and to make their rulings
effectual. Below the NLRB was a score of regional boards. So,
by trial and error, an industrial common law of collective
bargaining was hammered out.

But not at once. For there was no bridging the opinion gap
between employers and unions as to the permissible types of
bargaining unit. The NRA code system, in both its framing and
administration, subordinated union to management – as was
apparent from the fact that by April 1935 some $2\frac{1}{2}$m. workers
were in company unions, of whom between 60% and 70% had
arrived there since January 1933. Code enforcement, even when
the NLRB had reported offending employers to the Department
of Justice, was a constitutionally delicate affair. Long before the
Supreme Court (by the *Schechter* judgment of May 1935) invalidated the NRA and all its works, labour and liberal opinion
had come to regard Sections 7A and 8 as quite ineffectual, at
least for all but the strongest bargaining units. Beside an increasing militance, showing itself in bloody strikes like those of
San Francisco, Minneapolis and Toledo, unionism's only gain
from the 'National Run Around' was a wider experience of
countering recalcitrant employers at the bargaining table. But
the government, too, gained a clearer perception of what powers
its administrators needed for the same purpose.

Such experience stood the Administration in good stead when
it made the memorable decision not to amend the National
Recovery Act after *Schechter*, but to adopt in its place a privately sponsored bill which, strongly supported by the labour
lobby, had been buffeted around Congress for more than a year.
When on 5 July 1935 the President signed into law that land-
mark in American labour history, the National Labour Relations (Wagner) Act, he rendered unionism a service of the first
magnitude. The new measure roundly declared it to be in the
public interest 'to diminish the causes of labour disputes', and
that this was best done by permitting and encouraging free
association of workers for collective bargaining. It categorically
forbade certain 'unfair practices' by employers, in particular
discriminatory discharge, company unionism and refusal to

bargain. Section 7A was reiterated, expanded and provided with teeth.

The second National Labour Relations Board, set up by the Wagner Act, had learnt to conserve its strength. Eschewing mediation and arbitration, and taking no direct cognizance of wages, hours or working conditions as such, it concentrated upon 'unfair practices', union representation and the collective bargaining process itself, to which any issue arising out of the employer-employee relationship was regarded as germane. The Board now possessed authority to collect evidence, conduct hearings, make rulings and issue 'cease and desist' orders backed by threat of judicial proceedings.

But what support could the courts be relied on to give? The havoc notoriously wreaked by the Supreme Court upon the New Deal programme from 1935 to 1937, like its celebrated *volte face* of the latter year, requires mention here only insofar as it affected labour's attitude to and hopes from government. Having voided the Railroad Retirement Act and the Guffey Coal Act, on the respective grounds that neither railwaymen's pensions nor miners' hours bore close enough relevance to interstate commerce (*Railroad Retirement Board v. Alton Railroad* (1935); *Carter v. Carter Coal Co.* (1936)), the Court went on to strike down attempts by individual states to set minimum wages for women and children in industry. 'I defy anyone,' protested Roosevelt in March 1937, 'to read the opinions . . . and tell us exactly what, if anything, we can do for the industrial worker in this session of the Congress with any reasonable certainty that what we do will not be nullified as unconstitutional.'

The President's words were no more likely to pass unnoticed by the Court for being uttered at a Democratic dinner celebrating the biggest electoral victory any American party had ever enjoyed. A rise of nearly 6m. above the polling figures of 1932 had carried every state for Roosevelt save New Hampshire and Vermont, and all cities of 100,000 inhabitants or more; and it was reckoned that 5 out of every 6 new voters had given him their ballots. Of industrial states, in New York, New Jersey and Pennsylvania alone the Democratic vote had leapt by about 1·8m., and one scrutinizer of the returns had demonstrated that in almost every major city of the United States the Republican-Democrat voting division broke along a horizontal economic line which remained level despite topographical and racial diversities and irrespective of the area's past political tradition. An entire economic class had given Roosevelt a majority of more than 3 to 1 in the House and more than 4 to 1 in the Senate. Labour had acknowledged its debts.

The ensuing return of a 'self-reconstructed' Court to the tradition of Marshall, Story and Holmes was decisive in the sense that never again since that *annus mirabilis* has it held federal regulatory legislation of a major sort repugnant to the Constitution. When a lower court upheld the railroad retirement measure as remoulded by Congress, the high bench refused to intervene. Thereby it implicitly accepted – what much of the New Deal rested upon – that Congress might use the proceeds of federal taxation for anything which, whether covered by express or implied powers or neither, could reasonably be considered to be for the general welfare. On 24 May 1937 the Court handed down three rulings which sustained respectively an unemployment insurance law of the state of Alabama, the federal unemployment tax and the federal old age tax of the Social Security Act, as coming within the new and broadened concept of that welfare. Henceforward, in circumstances where it had no right directly to legislate, Congress might nevertheless use tax funds to induce the labour policy it desired. As for the police power of the states, where previously it had upset their minimum wage statutes by 5 to 4, the Court by another 5/4 decision in 1937 reversed itself (*West Coast Hotel Co. v. Parrish*) so as to allow Congress power to regulate wages and conditions of work for women and minors. But its most spectacular change of direction was performed in the spring of 1937, when in a series of five cases (the most notable of which was *N.L.R.B. v. Jones & Laughlin Steel Corporation*) the Court upheld the Wagner Act at all contested points. Thereafter, until world war supervened, it upheld also the NLRB's rulings in most cases arising out of complaints alleging discrimination by employers.

The *Jones & Laughlin* judgment in particular signified the judiciary's readiness at last to move away from the old formalistic interpretation of interstate commerce and towards a much more fluid notion that in practice legitimated the NLRB's intervention in virtually all labour disputes. By 1941, when upholding unanimously the Fair Labour Standards Act of 1938, the Court in effect announced that the judiciary would place no restriction on how the legislature used its own judgment in regulating such commerce, thus making the prohibition of child labour at last a reality. Reality was also given judicially to labour's right to strike and to picket in a seemingly ever-widening range of circumstances. Was this freedom becoming excessive? An academic lawyer, Thurman Arnold, placed at the head of the Department of Justice's antitrust division in the late 1930s, tried briefly and vigorously to practise his belief that Congress had not intended to exempt trade unions entirely from legislation forbidding 'unreasonable restraint' of commerce. But the highest bench could not be brought round to his way of thinking, and unionism remained legally free to take advantage of its recent growth in sheer numbers.

This growth, which was partly a regrowth, had begun haltingly. So sluggish was unionism's response to the new and favourable climate that by 1936 total paid-up membership was barely back to its 1920 strength. Pointing out that the unions to make the most successful recovery during the twenty-two months of the NRA's life were those willing to expand in complete disregard of craft partitions, Lewis, Hillman, Dubinsky and other leaders of the semi-skilled accused the craft hierarchs in the AFL of dragging their feet, of sleeping at the switch, and of letting slip the new and golden opportunities. The inchoate mass of new workers awaited a call which the old AFL leadership was doubly inhibited, by principles and by structure, from sounding. Its voluntarism demanded that the impulse towards organization must come not by superimposition from without but from the workers themselves. Its power resided in and was exercised through the officers of its craft internationals, who possessed well-developed instincts of legitimacy. And no device of the national executive – whether the old one of trades departments or the very recent one of federated multi-craft units – availed to resolve the problem of how to organize the unskilled now hammering on its door, without encroaching upon the longer established and jealously defended jurisdictions of the skilled.

Exasperated by the AFL's repeated failures either itself to harness the new potential or to countenance a broad movement of labour on a non-craft basis, the aggressive and ambitious leaders of the new unionism, though at first without thought of secession, took matters into their own hands. The protractedly painful process of fission, which occupied the three-and-a-half years between the defeat of a compromise resolution on industrial unionism at the 1934 convention and the AFL's revocation of the charters of dissident internationals in the spring of 1938, has been frequently recounted in detail. It is enough here to say that when in November of the latter year, at Pittsburgh, 32 disaffected national unions with state and city bodies, representing in all nearly 4m. unionists, entitled themselves the Congress of Industrial Organizations, a period of schism was inaugurated which was to last for another 17 years. Dual authority had reared its head from within the movement. Labour's self-government on the Gompersian model had broken down.

Long before the schism was complete, however, it had become evident that by their action the secessionists had demolished the barrier between organization and the unskilled. The year 1937 alone added more than 3m. to union membership, bringing it to a total of 2m. above the previous 1920 peak: by the end of it the unions of the future CIO had a bigger membership than the old AFL unions, and the percentage of industrial unionization had risen to over 50% of the combined total of 7½m. These new workers, in some areas demanding to be organized faster than the CIO could find recruiting agents, were swept in by the new body in a series of spectacular campaigns which began early in 1936 with a six-week strike at Akron and cut smoking swathes down the Ohio and Monongahela rivers. In the following June the CIO formed the Steel Workers' Organizing Committee, later to become the United Steel Workers of America. In 'Big Steel' the capitulation of management was swift, accompanied by few strikes, and the compact signed by Lewis with Myron C. Taylor of US Steel stole the main headlines of 1 March 1937. But in 'Little Steel' (five of the larger producers who did not follow the policies of US Steel) attack and defence both wore a para-military appearance and agreement was not reached without bloodshed, notably in the Memorial Day 'massacre' at the South Chicago plant of the Republican Steel Company in June of the most turbulent year that American industry has yet known.

In autos, union organizers faced a young and self-confident

industry, 90% of whose output was controlled by three firms. But by April 1937, after sit-down (or stay-in) strikes attended with the greatest publicity, General Motors and Chrysler had signed agreements, Detroit – the most aggressively anti-union city of the north – had been captured, and the United Automobile Workers had over $\frac{1}{4}$m. members. Ford held out till 1941. In textiles the Textile Workers' Organizing Committee under Hillman faced a heterogeneous industry where frontal attack would have availed little and chief reliance must be reposed in reasonableness and statistics. But the Ladies Garment Workers (ILGWU), though almost bankrupt, in one great strike shut down the dress industry and quintupled its own membership.

In another way, too, the CIO's secession promoted the growth of unionism, by making a fighting body of the parent federation. For the AFL was forced to compete with its upstart rival in new fields. Under stress of this competition many of its old craft unions at last expanded their jurisdictions to take in other workers than skilled, and a few more AFL units beside mining began to function on an industrial basis. An index of this new militance was that in 1941 the Federation was responsible for more strike calls than the CIO, despite the fact that the latter contained nearly 70% of the nation's strikers of that year.

This burst of economic expansion, being the clear result of a new governmental benignity ('Roosevelt wants you to join'), was not surprisingly accompanied by a marked resurgence of political activity, most immediately felt in the spheres of local and state government. The United Mine Workers captured mining communities and filled entire police forces with union members. The same union elected its international secretary-treasurer, Thomas Kennedy, to the lieutenant-governorship of Pennsylvania coincidentally with their big organizing drives in that state. While the biggest strike in American maritime history tied up all shipping on the Pacific Coast, the president of the Teamsters, Dave Beck, ruled Seattle through his protégé as chief of police. Labour votes ensured the return to office of sympathetic Governors in Michigan, Pennsylvania and Indiana. The last of these, when public feeling was running high over the sit-down strikes, saw to it that for the first time in American history troops were used not to disperse but to protect the strikers.

But it was on the national scale that labour's quickened appreciation of the importance of politics was naturally most conspicuous. Even before the discontented unions had set up house on their own, their leaders had devised means by which united labour would channel electoral support for its benefactor, the New Deal Administration (in sharp distinction from the Democratic party as a whole). On 10 August 1936 Labour's Non-Partisan League opened a Washington office with a full-time staff, and in the autumn elections its expenditure, direct and indirect, on Roosevelt's behalf exceeded by much all that the national AFL had spent on electoral activity since 1902. At a juncture when the Democrats found themselves cut off from many normal sources of campaign money, three CIO unions between them contributed $770,000 out of their general funds to the party of Roosevelt, including nearly $500,000 from Lewis's Mineworkers.

The League did not try to make itself the nucleus of a wider liberal movement. In New York, however, the state section of the League was virtually the American Labour Party, under whose banner liberals and left-of-liberals might vote for Roose-velt as distinct from Tammany Hall. Built up by Hillman and Dubinsky upon the foundation of the needle trade unions, the party's influence was chiefly but not entirely inspissated in New York city and its environs. The ALP supported Roosevelt in 1936, 1940 and 1944; in 1937 it joined with Republicans and anti-Tammany Democrats to return the incumbent Mayor Fiorello La Guardia, of whose majority the 1½m. votes cast on the ALP ticket represented about 35%; and at the same time the party elected five members of the City Council and five to the State Assembly. In 1942 it unsuccessfully ran its own candidate for governor; seemingly it could poll an impressive vote only when supporting a big figure.

Labour's Non-Partisan League at birth contained representatives of many of the old AFL unions, was headed by one of their presidents and enjoyed the support of the Railroad Brotherhoods. Yet in personnel and purpose it was so distinctly more typical of the CIO as to be borne away by the seceders. The AFL convention of 1937 excommunicated the League: a sure sign that major disagreements within the House of Labour over economic organization – by craft or industry? – must entail a basic divergence of opinion about the proper functions of government. The brunt of the depression had been borne by the lower-paid mass industry workers. The comparatively sheltered craft leadership of the AFL persisted in viewing 'statism' as the enemy. Pre-natal shock disposed the CIO, by contrast, to think in terms of a broad and permanent policy of security for the mass industry workers out of whose myriad small dues, sharply sensitive to the national economic index, its treasury was compiled. The AFL's roots were in the localities: the CIO industries from the first were battlegrounds of inter-regional competition, where undesirable disparities in wage levels and in labour codes could be ironed out only under pressure from Washington. The AFL publicly deplored the notoriety into which the CIO's sit-down strikes had plunged the labour movement, and advocated forcible suppression of the young organizers. The CIO retorted by accusing the older federation of playing the employers' game by failing to repel the latter's attacks on the New Deal legislation which had provided the legal basis for labour's mass organizing drives, but was now coming under fire from the conservative coalition returned to Congress by the mid-term elections of 1938. As *rapport* between the CIO and the Administration grew closer, the AFL in those elections had given its cachet to a large number of Republican candidates, not for their pro-labour record but for their resistance to the CIO.

By that year the two competing federations had evolved two opposing power structures. When Lewis, who had supported Coolidge in 1924 and Hoover in 1928, returned dramatically to his old Republican allegiance in 1940, the AFL had plausible grounds for asserting that their rivals were politically dominated by the vaulting ambition of the Mineworkers' leader. In the event, however, Lewis was reckoned to have swung at the most only 2% of workers with him; and Roosevelt, though with a reduced majority, ran in the CIO regions well ahead of his national lead. Nevertheless, and although the falling-off of the labour vote in 1940 was not great even where it was greatest (in Pennsylvania), a Gallup poll taken shortly after the election revealed a distinct decline from 1936 in the Roosevelt vote of every labour group. The overall margin of Roosevelt and his running mate, Henry A. Wallace, was dangerously narrow, and in New York state less than ¼m. votes. Here and in six other industrialized states Rooseveltian percentages varied between 51·2 and 53·5. These seven states, with a total of 209 votes in the electoral college, contained nearly 9m. of the 30m. American non-voters, and a little more than 1m. ballots there would have given victory to the Republicans. CIO voters being strategically distributed all over this area, it is not hard to believe that Lewis would have had to carry less than a quarter of them with him to have handed the election to Willkie. With Lewis's estrangement from his colleagues the League declined, and when early in the war he and his union left the CIO fold there remained of it merely a political arm of the Mineworkers.

Though labour's political front had held firm in 1940, it soon became evident that the tide of reform had turned. The ebb was partly a general reaction against the New Deal, partly a waning sympathy for unionism caused by exasperation at its civil wars and by alarm at the CIO's militant organizing tactics. The feeling in Congress that unionism had by 1938 received its just deserts was apparent in the lukewarm reaction to the La Follette subcommittee's reports, whose horrifying disclosures of the continued use by employers of violence and espionage in labour relations left legislators comparatively unmoved. The total number of American trade unionists in 1940 was almost at the 9m. mark (of whom nearly 4·3m. were in the AFL, over 3·6m. in the CIO, and over 1m. in independent bodies). Was not labour getting too big for its boots?

Positively the year 1938 saw the beginnings of a crescendo of hostility to the Wagner Act and the NLRB. Of the many unfriendly proposals before the Seventy-Sixth Congress, some wanted to modify the Act so as to reduce its coverage by defining certain classes of worker (e.g. the agricultural labourer) in such a way as to exempt them from the Act's provisions; or by withdrawing certain cases from its jurisdiction (such as disputes between labour units having a common affiliation). Others would amend the Act in the employer's favour by enlarging his freedom to persuade (short of coercive interference), to 'counsel and advise' in matters of labour organization, or even to favour (other than by pecuniary means) one labour organization against another; or by redefining collective bargaining so as to categorize 'unfair labour practices' of unions as well as management. Still other bills proposed to reduce the NLRB's jurisdiction by transferring some of its functions to the courts; by depriving it of discretion to determine the appropriate bargaining unit; or even by displacing it with an entirely new Board. The AFL itself adopted in convention a 9–point programme for reforming the Board so as to make it an instrument of self-preservation for the craft unions.

But to all these attempts to debilitate the Wagner Act the best defence proved to be the plain facts and figures of the NLRB's annual reports. Their record of overwhelming success ensured that when the sands of world peace ran out the Wagner Act remained unrepealed and unamended. Yet something had been exacted by way of ransom: the Board paid it by reforming its membership and procedures in a conservative sense. Meanwhile in the states a number of legislatures were whittling away some of the benefits conferred on workers by the federal parliament. Here again the internal conflicts of unionism must be held in part responsible: if Oregon and California reduced the employee's freedom to strike it was under severe provocation from the civil war being waged along their coasts by longshoremen's and maritime unions.

The year 1938, which saw the last instalment of New Deal labour legislation, is a convenient point from which to survey from our particular angle what Charles A. Beard called the second, and others have called the third, American revolution. In its opening passages, which were a desperate search for ways and means, the goodwill of the new Administration was not sharply focused upon unions as such. Rather the goal was proclaimed to be 'a true concert of interests'. But failure of the NRA to achieve it was succeeded by a swing to the left perceptible by the middle of 1935, when the President's first set of advisers had been displaced by the second, and when those sections of the NRA favourable to business were not re-enacted. There followed a seeming retreat from the concept of non-competitive 'public interest' to the narrower but more familiar ground of competing special interests, among which organized labour was prominent. Economic recovery, sustained up to and over the recession of 1937–8, left a resuscitated trade union movement which found itself inhabiting a pluralistic or mixed economy. It was also a managed economy, but the prevailing tone was audibly one of state capitalism, not state socialism.

To the New Deal as a whole, or to a series of new deals in sum, unionism owed first and foremost a decade of uninterrupted growth in numbers, in scope, in wealth and in influence. The 12m. union members of 1942 represented a higher proportion of the national labour force than ever before organized. Not only had unionism penetrated to the mass industries and to certain groups of white collar workers – retail clerks, office workers and newspaper reporters – but it had spread outside its normal urban habitat into middle-sized and small manufacturing communities, and had made some headway among cannery workers, agricultural hired hands and even sharecroppers. The growing industrial centres of the south had been invaded for the first time; in Kentucky the UMW, with some help from the NLRB, had at last tamed 'bloody Harlan county'. By 1940, the attitude of the AFL's agents having made a complete turn from exclusiveness to inclusiveness, the percentage of unionists organized on a craft basis had dropped below ten.

During the same period the right of association for collective bargaining was written into the law of the land. By 1943 it determined conditions of employment in most basic American industries, where its tendency was towards written agreements of wider geographical coverage. From one of the most restrictive among industrially advanced nations, the labour code of the United States (insofar as it could be said to exist before 1933) was rapidly transformed into one of the most liberal. The combination of workers in industry had gained the recognition and protection of the courts, an impressive rise in real wages, and a welfare service which promised to ramify into every area of social need. Policies that were wise for labour and policies that were good for the public came to appear almost identical. The labour movement, it might be said, had at last been woven into the fabric of American culture. And all this had been done without picking the fabric to pieces. For the President worked to rehabilitate and re-fortify an economic order which, as a close colleague of his has written, he took as much for granted as he did his own family.

It cannot so confidently be said that these legislative gains were the fruit of labour's own efforts. The bankruptcy of labour philosophy in the face of depression had left a vacuum to be filled by radicals – the National Unemployment League, the Workers' Alliance of America, and others – whose members were later to aid the organizational drives of the CIO. Even after three years of depression the AFL's leaders continued to rely on skilled labour shortage to push their craftsmen's bargaining power up. William Green, Gompers's successor as AFL president, a lay ex-preacher and the embodiment of all that is signified by non-controversial, in 1933 was still uttering hollow threats that unionism might exercise its 'economic force, . . . the only language that a lot of employers ever understand'. Relief in the form of WPA projects they viewed with suspicion as likely to permit lower rates for the job. Nor did the Federation, lacking any specialized staff in that field, have much to do with development of the Administration's social security programmes. Indeed, the AFL's prevalent fear was lest unemployment insurance plans might too closely resemble the British, regarded as mere compensation for enforced idleness. It was Frances Perkins, Roosevelt's humane Secretary of Labour, who injected the minimum wage component, union leaders being more concerned with maximum hours. The AFL, in fact, were tending to support the contraction of industry by a shorter working week, as opposed to the Administration's objective of expansion through increased purchasing power. Although Walsh-Healey did have wholehearted labour support, it was the series of objections raised by unionism that almost shipwrecked the Fair Labour Standards Act of 1938 in committee.

The reforms of 1933–38, then, were not the harvest of long-sustained agitation by trade unions, but were forced upon a partly sceptical labour movement by a government which led or carried it into maturity. To what organ of that government were American workers most indebted? Without doubt the shaping and planning forces behind concrete social and labour legislation were to be found on Capitol Hill rather than in the White House. The Norris-La Guardia Act, the Wagner Act, and its precursor the Railroad Labour Act of 1934, all originated among liberal members of Congressional committees, and were passed by considerable majorities. Of privately sponsored measures, the Wagner Act was to give to American labour relations the statutory basis which, though significantly amended in 1947, largely prevails today. If it did not immediately diminish, but rather augment, industrial strife, this was because of the long-term benefits it seemed to hold out to unions prepared to take advantage of it. By encouraging collective bargaining it opened the way to the growth of a large and independent labour movement. Though by the end of the New Deal the recognition it received from employers was far from universal – only about one-third of manufacturing employees were trade union members by 1940 – yet this led to a wider recognition of that movement as a natural and desirable feature of American society. Through administrative interpretation of the collective bargaining contract, the Act led also in time to a peculiarly American form of legalistic co-determination in industry. And by relating that contract to majority decisions within a plant, it fostered as much democratic participation as workers anywhere are disposed to show.

What did labour owe the President? While Roosevelt's attitude towards workers as a whole was manifestly compassionate, his sympathy for organized labour was politically conditioned. Workers had votes, whether organized or not. To improve the wage-earner's lot was, up to a point, good politics: but adequate public support was a precondition for adopting a measure such as the Wagner Act. Though indifferent to unionism's technical problems, and frequently exasperated by its strikes and civil war, he was as a politician acutely conscious of labour as a necessary counterweight to the autocracy of business. As workers became increasingly beholden to the Administration, so the Administration became increasingly aware of the electoral advantage of giving hospitality to labour's viewpoint. And that viewpoint tended increasingly to be the CIO's rather than the AFL's. In turn, workers in the mass came more and more to regard the political process as a ready and natural channel for realizing their aspirations.

For the great change wrought upon the American system by the first two Rooseveltian terms was of course that in its working the government took a part and that the greatest. The consequences, apparent on every side, are revealed most simply and directly by a consideration of the amount of money pumped into it in the form of relief. In the fiscal year 1939–40, after six years of reconstruction, 27·1 % of all governmental expenditure was for public aid. But relief was only a small detail of a large canvas. Government's permissible power was now much wider. If it was to mitigate depression it must be free also to regulate the business conditions precedent to depression, the boom as well as the bust. If it were to take responsibility for the downward swings it must have responsibility for the movement in its entirety. Power to plan for one part of the economy logically entailed power to plan for the whole.

How far the new government had intruded into that segment of the economy occupied by labour-management relations was already partially apprehended on both sides of the bargaining table. Clearly, in setting minimum standards Congress had signalled the end of that period when management alone decided how many hours its men were to work, in what physical conditions, and for what wages. It was less clear what would be the fate of these standards in the event of a national emergency (such as war) when governmental labour policy would be swayed by considerations external to the labour-management relationship (such as inflation). Again, it was evident that the Wagner Act had abrogated management's traditional freedom to grant or withhold recognition to associations of employees, to bargain or not to bargain with them. But other consequences of government's new proximity to unionism were less obvious. To adjudge between two or more rival groups claiming to represent the workers in a factory, the NLRB must apply extrinsic standards, tests of validity that were not necessarily labour's – the outcome of a plant plebiscite, for example, instead of the terms of a union's charter.

Any misgiving that labour might feel on this score was postponed to an immediate and much more vivid apprehension of advantages to be derived from the government's economic presence. Just as business would never again accept widespread bankruptcies nor farmers wholesale foreclosures and twenty-cent wheat as the law of nature, so American labour has since refused to tolerate governmental passivity in the face of unemployment, or to view a descending phase of the business cycle as an act of God. It has preferred to believe that economic crises are largely man-made and can be largely man-controlled, and that the best controlling machinery is in Washington. A ghost is still present when labour sits down to its convention feasts –

the ghost of 16m. unemployed. So long as one quarter of that number may be jobless, unionism looks to politics, as well as to its contracts, for guarantees of economic security and material welfare.

But the strongest pressure for changing labour's attitude towards political action came, not from economic doctrine or administrative benevolence, but from those millions of workers given access to unionism for the first time, the offspring of the 'new' post–1885 immigration, the climbing big city masses now come of voting age and representing a radically new political force. Uninhibited by the traditional outlook of the AFL, and recognizing their indebtedness to government, they found the old anti-statism unintelligible. Millions to whom 'natural economic laws' and 'rugged individualism' were incomprehensible were to attach themselves to the reforming party and to give its leaders, until 1952, overwhelming pluralities of the urban vote. Like every revolution, the New Deal generated power of a new kind. Though both the old parties retained their inclusive character and nationwide base, yet it was the Democrats, in their novel guise of social-service-minded centralizers, who tapped the new potential.

Finally, by politicizing so much of the nation's economic life, the New Deal forced the worker as citizen to become politically conscious and literate. For one thing, it left him less and less able to distinguish between what benefited him as trade unionist and what as citizen, for the new legislation touched him immediately in both capacities. His vistas were crowded not only by collective bargaining guarantees, maximum wages and minimum hours, but by deductions of social security taxes from payrolls, relief payments, benefit payments, marketing orders, bank deposit guarantees and home loans. For another, by bringing the government into the labour-management relationship, the New Deal opened the terms of that relationship to public discussion in the form of issues about which the citizen *qua* unionist was obliged to inform himself. How unionism has seized this opportunity to undertake the 'political education' of its members must be left for a later chapter to show. Between the revolution of the thirties and our own time another emergency intervenes, and one of more than purely national dimensions.

6

4

The new model of
Sidney Hillman

The most immediate consequence of war in Europe for labour
in America was a rapid march along the road to full employment. The first milestone was the President's announcement (16
May 1940) of the government's massive plans for defence production; the second, the 'arsenal of democracy' programme after
Congress's enactment of Lend-Lease on 11 March 1941; the
third, Roosevelt's proclamation of 27 May 1941 of an 'unlimited' national emergency, calling for a 24-hour-day, seven-
day-week in defence industries. The fourth was Pearl Harbour
itself, on the following 7 December. By then the Bureau of
Labour Statistics was reporting unemployment fallen to 5m.;
and thereafter the mean figure until 1945 never rose to 3% of the
civilian labour force. In one respect at least, war had accom-
plished what the New Deal had failed to do.

The second consequence of world conflict, as in all countries
involved, was to prolong and heighten the dominance of the
executive. This was manifest in the plethora of new and temporary agencies – 'offices', 'boards', 'administrations' – which
sprang into being at the President's behest. Their rulings, in
theory only 'advisory', were no less efficacious than statutory
sanctions, as both business and labour were to discover. Thus,
obstructiveness in some sections of the labour force, as when
certain building unions tried to maintain exclusive membership
practices or impede transfer of their members to war construction, could be remedied, and compliance with national wage

policies secured, by threats of deprival of union security (by the War Labour Board), or even of cancellation of workers' deferment from military service (by the War Manpower Commission). As the administration by successive twists tightened its hold, business found itself increasingly subject to priority orders, allocation of materials, price ceilings and high taxation; labour to a no-strike agreement, wage stabilization, and denial of mobility to better paying jobs.

Both were subject to regulation of manpower. But for that purpose Congress, unlike the British and Dominion parliaments, never resorted to statute, even under great Presidential pressure. Instead, main responsibility was vested in a War Manpower Commission, whose chairman possessed the wide powers and onerous responsibilities necessary for moving workers from inessential to essential jobs and keeping them there. Though occasionally compelled towards minatory public gestures, such as the 'work or fight' order of 3 February 1945, the Commission's use of a joint labour-management committee normally secured a grumbling acquiescence in its day-to-day policies.

On the whole, though, the problems which chiefly exercised American unions in war remained, though more intensely, those of peace – the settlement of disputes with management and the maintenance of union security. Immediately after Pearl Harbour the AFL endorsed its executive council's proposal for a no-strike policy in all defence production industries. In so doing it to some extent made a virtue of necessity, for public and Congressional feeling had for several years past been running strongly against unionism. Labour would rather be ruled by President than by Congress. When, therefore, Roosevelt in January 1942 summoned to Washington representatives of the AFL and CIO to confer for five days with representatives of industry, and shortly thereafter 'accepted' with 'congratulations' recommendations (which actually the conference never got within a mile of making) for a three-point programme to govern wartime labour relations – exchange by the two parties of no-strike, no-lockout pledges, a joint resolution to observe for the duration an armistice under which all settlements would be reached by peaceful means, the creation of a special agency to handle industrial disputes – labour stifled its misgivings about the delays inseparable from jurisdiction by a governmental agency, about the abeyance of collective bargaining as a solvent of routine problems, about the absence of machinery to reassign workers to new jobs, and deferred with as good grace as possible. In return it received from the President assurances that the gains embodied in the Wagner, Walsh-Healey and Wage-Hour Acts would not be placed in jeopardy; and it received the National War Labour Board.

A tripartite body of twelve Presidential appointees, the War Labour Board was set up on 12 January 1942 in the Office of Emergency Management with jurisdiction over all labour disputes certified to it by the Department of Labour as likely to hold up the effective prosecution of the war. It was soon recognized, by virtue of its capacity as 'adviser' to the President, as the real seat of authority over labour-management controversy, towards which the disputants advanced through the preliminary stages of formal negotiation with as much celerity as was decent. With the unions the Board was not at first unpopular; nor did the record of its three years of operation lack achievement – some 14,000 disputes adjudicated, in only twenty-five of which had governmental seizure been required to secure compliance. Enjoying equal representation with management and the public, labour secured equitable return for its forbearance in terms of union security through an evolving 'maintenance of membership' formula, which came after a time to be automatically applied upon a union's satisfying certain criteria of 'reasonable' behaviour. The trouble began when, in October 1942, Congress amended the price control mechanism so as to transform the WLB, almost overnight, into the government's chief wage stabilizing agency. Henceforth the Board and its regional offices appeared as the main barrier between the unions and the pay increases they sought.

In the wages field, as in that of union security, the coming of war had evoked from unionism a voluntary pledge of self-denial – again, an act of prudence, for many voices in Congress were being raised to demand compulsory suspension of the Wage-Hour law for the duration. From the beginning of 1943 onward a forty-eight-hour week was the basic standard in many defence industries. It was not labour shortage, however, but general inflation that eventually led wages – which, unlike prices and rents, had not been pegged by Congress – out of voluntarism into governmental control. In the *International Harvester Co.* decision of April 1942, the WLB warned that the need to combat inflation must have precedence over the cost-of-living factor, and that labour must not, therefore, 'expect to receive throughout the war upward changes in its wage structure which will enable it to keep pace with upward changes in the cost of living'. This new attitude of the Board found its most celebrated expression in the 'Little Steel Formula' of 16 July 1942, tying wage increases to the general increase in cost of living since 1 January 1941, which the Board put at 15%. Twice reinforced, by Congress and by President, this formula was held applicable to non-wage 'fringe' benefits also; and although Hillman warned Roosevelt personally that labour's dissatisfaction with it was 'practically unanimous', it remained an impenetrable barrier between unions and their goal. After the war, however, they were to revisit this battlefield of fringe benefits, and by then the WLB was dead.

Meanwhile it was John L. Lewis who led the assault. To understand both Lewis's aggressiveness and his unpopularity during these years, one needs to look back and see how his unhappy estrangement from Washington had come about. In his own eyes, his Mineworkers' big contribution to Roosevelt's 1936 campaign – 'cash on the barrel', Lewis called it, 'for every piece of legislation we [the CIO] have gotten' – had entitled him to greater esteem and consultation from the White House; perhaps (though he was not even a Democrat) to the Vice-Presidential nomination itself. Roosevelt showing less consideration than Lewis considered his due, their relationship had deteriorated to the climactic point of 25 October 1940, when Lewis dramatically went on the air from coast to coast, excoriating the nation's leader and coming out for Willkie. Upon the electoral outcome he staked his own CIO presidency. When the CIO, devoted to him economically, refused to follow him politically, Hillman at their next annual convention quietly took him at his word and secured the presidential succession for the unflamboyant Philip Murray. Upon Sidney Hillman himself, a Lithuanian immigrant who had risen through the needle trades unions to head the Amalgamated Clothing Workers, henceforward fell the mantle of labour statesmanship and national spokesmanship.

As Hillman's star waxed, so did Lewis's jealousy and monomania. In November 1941 he pulled the CIO's representatives out of the National Defence Mediation Board (a predecessor of the WLB for the purpose of industrial mediation) because it refused to order a union shop in the 'captive' mines of the steel industry. Having secured a reversal of its ruling, early in 1943 the Mineworkers' leader moved again, this time with a substantial wage demand from the coal operators. Their refusal to parley he then declared to be in violation of the Wagner Act, and declined to go before the WLB. There followed in dramatic succession a miners' walk-out, government seizure of the mines, a truce, another strike, and deferring of a final settlement until May 1944 – the whole series of events cast by the press into the form of a duel between the President and 'John L. Lewis – Hitler's Helper' of 'coal-black soul'. Congress, for its part, took from the files its blueprint for anti-strike legislation, and on 25 June 1943 the only labour statute of the war was signed by a reluctant President whose veto had been overridden by comfortable majorities.

The declared purpose of the War Labour Disputes (Smith-Connally) Act was to prevent industrial disputes which 'may lead to substantial interference with the war effort'. Where such a contingency threatened, it put Congress's authority behind Presidential seizure of plants and mines. It gave the War Labour Board a statutory basis. While not forbidding strikes, it imposed a mandatory thirty-day 'cooling-off' period, after which the National Labour Relations Board might hold a secret ballot to find whether the majority of workers favoured or opposed striking. In his veto message Roosevelt pointed to a no-strike record 'as good or better than the record of any of our allies in wartime', and warned that the bill would 'stimulate labour unrest and give government sanction to strike agitators'. But his Administration made no serious attempt to organize opposition on the floor.

'One of the most serious blows against our national war effort,' Murray of the CIO called Smith-Connally; and Green for the AFL threatened rebellion if it were passed. In the event labour did not rebel, did not even withdraw from the WLB: for Smith-Connally proved inefficacious. Six months after its passage the total time lost in strikes, though still minute, was higher than at any previous wartime juncture. Indeed, the opportunity of an NLRB-conducted poll probably weakened the no-strike pledge by putting an official channel at the disposal of the dissatisfied worker, by providing Lewis and other leaders with huge and public votes of confidence from their followers, and by seeming to deny government the moral right to seize a polled mine or plant thereafter. So too often the filing of a notice of intent to strike became a recognized tactic in labour relations, and the cooling-off period one of warming-up. In the first year of Smith-Connally's operation the Secretary of Labour received more than a thousand strike notices. In December 1945, after the NLRB had spent $200,000 of public funds in polling the UMW to discover that Lewis's men favoured a strike by 8 to 1, Congress forbade the Board to spend any more money on such elections, and shortly afterwards Truman declared that function extinct. The whole Act expired on 30 June 1947.

It remains to add that, unlike Congress, the federal courts showed in wartime no inclination to withdraw from labour the benignity they had so recently come to display. On the contrary, their general trend was to amplify it. In a series of decisions the Supreme Court expanded its interpretation of inter-state commerce so as to bring new categories of worker under the Fair Labour Standards Act. At the same time it somewhat extended the meaning of 'employee' in the Wagner Act; showed increasing indulgence to unions when interpreting 'restraint of trade' under the Sherman Act; and in one case (*Hunt v. Crombach*, 1945) appeared to legitimize boycotting conducted by a union, not in pursuit of improved wages or working conditions, but to force a non-unionized employer out of business. A view of the Sherman and Norris-La Guardia Acts so broad as almost totally to immunize unions from anti-trust prosecution disquieted even liberals, and strengthened feeling in Congress that future legislation in this area must be given some minimal relevance to organized labour.

With the United States in its third year of hostilities, union leaders were beginning to find it both possible and desirable to cast a rough balance sheet of labour's gains and losses.

Among the chief gains was the extent – greater than in World War I – to which they themselves had been brought into national policy-making. To all major sections of the federal government the need to consult and maintain good relations with organized labour was obvious. The latter's right to participate directly and formally in policy-making had indeed been recognized before the USA was even at war. Immediately after the capitulation of France, on 28 May 1940, Roosevelt announced the formation of a National Defence Council. This parent of all subsequent wartime production and control agencies was to be advised upon the problems of defence mobilization by a small commission, among whom was Sidney Hillman, president of the Amalgamated Clothing Workers of America (CIO). Hillman's tasks at the head of the NDC's labour division were to maintain good labour-management relations in war industries, to uphold the labour standards of the New Deal, to assess and equate demand and supply of skilled labour, and to supervise the training and accommodation of war workers. 'Sidney,' Roosevelt is reported to have said, 'I want you to keep labour in step'; and in his capacity of chief personnel manager to the government Hillman selected to advise him a joint board of union representatives, six from the AFL, six from the CIO, and four from the Railroad Brotherhoods.

The Commission's staff had grown to 1,500, of whom Hillman's division employed about one fifth, when at the end of 1940 its duties passed to a new body with greatly strengthened powers. In the Office of Production Management Hillman henceforward shared authority with William S. Knudsen, president of General Motors; and in mediating disputes during a period of spreading industrial unrest before the no-strike pledge was given, this two-headed organization did work of considerable importance. Mediation in a particularly bloody and costly strike at the Allis-Chalmers plant in Milwaukee induced Hillman to propose and assist in the erection of a tripartite National Defence Mediation Board which included top union officials. Until disrupted by Lewis, who was not a member, the NDMB relieved the Department of Labour of its conciliation duties in defence industry. One way and another, Hillman reflected, 'every department of government affecting labour in defence came under my jurisdiction'.

So long as the OPM lasted – which was less than eighteen months – labour possessed on the very highest plane of emergency administration a representative whose power to give or withhold contracts was, as even the mighty Henry Ford soon learned, power of economic life or death. The Office's unpopularity, however, with a nation not yet itself involved in hostilities was manifested in the sustained barrage of criticism from Congress, the business community and the press; and when war came, the sharpened problem of controlling the civilian labour force called for reconsideration. After three months of uncertainty Roosevelt referred it for solution to a new body, the War Manpower Commission.

With the supersession of Hillman, labour's influence in Washington, and with the President in particular, underwent a sharp decline. Throughout a vast administrative range – containing the War Manpower Commission, the War Production Board, the Office of Price Administration, the Economic Stabilization Board and later the Office of War Mobilization and Reconversion, and of course the War Labour Board – organized labour indeed continued to make its influence felt. Yet this range was well below the political summit. And it may be doubted whether labour's representatives always made the most of the temporary eminence they enjoyed. There was evidence that only too often appointments to a government agency and its regional panels were regarded by the union hierarchy as a form of patronage with which to reward union dignitaries irrespective of their capacity as negotiators. Many such representatives, particularly top officers like Green and Murray, were unable to devote sufficient time to work that became increasingly technical. Others were not always supplied by their unions with adequate facts and figures when facing the well-briefed representatives of the National Association of Manufacturers or U.S. Chamber of Commerce.

Labour indeed claimed, and was accorded, formal partnership in the government of the country. But the impression remains that it was the symbol of participation, rather than the substance, that was really coveted; that unionism's demand to be consulted wherever relevant decisions were taken did not mean that it always had ready a reasoned case for presentation or uniquely competent spokesmen to present it. Correspondingly, the lack of concern displayed by some administrator when no positive recommendations were forthcoming from his labour advisers, or the inclination of an agency chairman to embark on policies without prior consultation with the workers' accredited representatives, did not necessarily argue his lack of receptivity to 'the official labour view'. It was at least as likely that he had come to accept the presence of union spokesmen at the valuation which they themselves had set upon it – not much more than one of prestige.

Comparison with wartime Britain, where labour leaders sat clothed with the fullness of authority in a coalition government, leads to the ineluctable conclusion that unionism in America was doing poorly in relation to its potentialities. It was without a voice in the cabinet. If Hillman himself, as his biographer tells us, by special permission often entered the White House by the back door, he owed this freedom to his personal relationship with the occupant and not to any solidarity of support from union officialdom outside. As a prime seceder he was obnoxious to the AFL, and scarcely more popular with some sections of the CIO until Lewis took his Mineworkers out of it in October 1942. When the OPM was wound up, few beyond Hillman's own Clothing Workers mourned the disappearance from Washington of labour's only politician of the first rank. On tripartite bodies, labour's votes tended to be paired off against those of industry, leaving the trick to be turned by representatives of the public. And to the public, for whom Lewis personified labour's acquisitive spirit, the diligence and restraint of most unionists were less evident than the jealousies dividing them.

A solider item on the credit side were labour's more conventional wartime gains. Despite official freezes, wage-earners had enjoyed a faster rise in income than any other American social group except farmers; an improvement which the success of the government's stabilization policy in the last two years of the war made a reality. From the conflict the unions emerged with union security preserved (through various 'maintenance of membership' formulae devised by the War Labour Board: see note at p. 99 below) and with federal labour legislation almost unimpaired. Membership had spread. Out of a civilian labour force of over 51m. (one-third of them women) at the end of 1944, about three-tenths belonged either to AFL or CIO, and included industrial categories never before organized. In 1919 union members had numbered scarcely 5m.: when peace came in 1945 they were over 15m. strong. Moreover, the wartime need for uninterrupted production allowed collective bargaining to penetrate regions hitherto reserved to managerial prerogative. To do so in the context of tripartite bodies required, as we have seen, a substantial and orderly presentation of briefs: hence many unions emerged from the war with economic, research and legal divisions greatly fortified in size and expertise. Again, the centralizing tendency of wartime bargaining induced the practice of negotiating in industry-wide terms; a trend advantageous to labour as favouring both the concentration of a union's bargaining strength and the ironing-out of regional inequalities in wages and working conditions.

On the other side of the ledger, fears for the future disposed labour to self-defence rather than attack. In the first place, it was hard to see how the immediate post-war period could be other than one of rapid retrenchment, however gradually a swollen work-force was reabsorbed into peacetime occupations. Peace would see the termination of defence contracts aggregating billions of dollars. How many jobs could private industry offer when government withdrew? Cutbacks were freely predicted which would take between 6m. and 8m. men and women out of work by the spring of 1946. The best official advice the AFL could get was that it would be impossible to avoid severe unemployment, say 7m. workless, for a transitional period of two years without some kind of public works programme.

A government at war, moreover, had virtually underwritten employers' wage bills. When industrialists, undertaking reconversion without benefit of government subsidies, resumed cost-conscious competition in a free labour market, unions would surely face, as in the 1930s, a choice between pay-cuts and shutdowns. Again, wartime investment had made the government owner of between $15b. and $20b. worth of plant and equipment – a new form of public domain as important as the western lands had been a century before. Much of this was deliberately sited in hitherto thinly-industrialized areas, such as the South, normally of low wages and sparse unionization. Was it all to be handed over to business, to retain or shut down at its own discretion?

More than this, reconversion would involve the redeployment, geographical as well as technological, of some twenty million workers, not to mention the reabsorption of returning war veterans. Unionism, therefore, faced a tremendous shake-up of membership and affiliation; and this at a time when the two major labour federations remained bitter rivals, and when the vast number of their wartime recruits had lacked the opportunity to become familiar with those traditional peacetime bargaining methods to which unions must now revert. For four years intervention by federal agencies had largely displaced across-the-table negotiation. The War Labour Board (to cite only one instance) had been confirmed by the Smith-Connally Act in its authority 'to decide the dispute and provide by order the wages and hours *and all other terms and conditions governing the relations between*' employers and employed. Union security itself had been made subject to governmental scrutiny of a local's (that is to say, a branch's) internal affairs in order to ascertain whether these satisfied certain conditions: whether, for example, it fairly represented the interests of all (including non-union and minority-union) workers in a plant, refrained from racial discrimination, etc. Of the union leaders themselves, compelled in recent years to justify government policy to a restless rank and file, many of the more experienced had paid the price of their moderation by defeat in union elections.

Not only, then, would collective bargaining in all its pre-war vitality be difficult of early restoration, but it had become the case that unions, as protégés of federal statute, must submit to a degree of federal regulation. Through the National Labour Relations Board they had received the government's cachet, and they must recognize that power to issue a certificate subsumed power to make conditions and to ensure they were observed. The Board's certificate had thus become a badge of legitimacy almost as essential to a union as its charter from the parent association. The breach thereby made in the old wall of union self-government would never again be fully closed.

These many considerations all combined to convince American labour, viewing the future at any time from 1943 onwards, of the need for political engagement on a scale and with a consistency never before contemplated. War had revealed some of the blessings flowing from a controlled economy. Certain tangible rewards – full employment, marvellous increases in productivity and, despite abnormal economic conditions, a fair stability of prices – were demonstrably attainable by planning. With such gains at stake, the many problems of post-war industrial life could not be returned for solution to the spontaneity of competitive business. At the same time, unionism was not strong enough to tackle them unaided. Any abrupt and unplanned transition from a controlled to a de-controlled economy might throw it back to the position it had occupied in respect of management in 1919. The post-war choice for labour was not whether government should or should not be actively concerned with the labour scene. Given the desirability of governmental intervention, the questions were rather to what degree and for what ends? 'Disaster,' Philip Murray warned, 'comes by accident, but prosperity comes only by planning'; and the only planning agency in which he and his colleagues could place any confidence was the government's. In 1943, accordingly, the CIO set up within its Department of Research and Education a Post-War Planning Committee which in January 1944 issued the first of a series of reports developing a seminal theme: – 'Post war plans must be based on clear-cut recognition of the responsibility of the federal government for securing and maintaining full employment, production and consumption.' The AFL, though less whole-heartedly in favour of continuing government intervention, was taking comparable steps of its own.

Another problem naturally followed from this. At what point could pressure be best applied to government, and by what means? Labour could hope for little from the Seventy-Eighth Congress, where the mid-term elections of 1942 had reduced Democratic majorities to their lowest levels since 1933. The heavy casualties suffered by liberals, and the large number of Democratic votes cast to override the President's veto of Smith-Connally, suggested that in domestic affairs Roosevelt could no longer control his own party. With regard to the burning topic of reconversion Congressional action had been retrogressive. When in 1943 the last of the New Deal's major planning agencies, the National Resources Planning Board, submitted in two massive reports its plans for full production and full employment in peacetime, Congress hastily wound the Board up, forbidding the President to transfer any of its functions to any other agency; and in its stead each House created its own

Special Committee on Post-war Economic Policy and Planning, predominantly conservative in composition. Twelve months later Roosevelt asked Congress to appropriate $76m. for the planning of public works construction; Congress appropriated $5m. Labour's feelings were summed up by one of the many CIO pamphlets of the time:

> A Congress which refuses to back the President in his
> program in the interests of the people, a Congress which
> votes against labour, against taxes according to ability to
> pay, against food subsidies and real price control, against
> the home front programme to win the war quickly and
> effectively: – such a Congress cannot be entrusted with
> writing the peace or ensuring jobs and security in the postwar
> period.

Turning from Congress to the Administration, the prospect seemed little more reassuring. Again it was clear that the economic problems of the immediate future would have to be grappled with in a climate very different from that of ten years earlier. Having assumed the stupendous burden of foreign relations, Roosevelt had largely delegated to other men the task of maintaining liaison with Congress in the framing of domestic policies. These new men labour did not count as friends. On 3 October 1943 Congress had set up an Office of War Mobilization and Reconversion – all that remained of far-reaching proposals for an agency with responsibility for planning full production, full employment and an extensive scheme of compensation for the unavoidably unemployed. But after Roosevelt had in October 1942 taken James F. Byrnes off the Supreme Court in order to make him Director of Economic Stabilization and 'Assistant President' with an office in the White House, and still more after Byrnes had brought in, among other anti-New Dealers, Fred M. Vinson as Economic Stabilizer and Director of OWMR, complaints were loud that labour was being given no real opportunity to influence the policies of the new Office. Though thirty-two other agencies were believed also to be planning the post-war economy, not one spokesman contradicted predictions of a 40% cutback in production immediately after VE-Day. While in Britain a White Paper (from the Ministry of Reconstruction, entitled *Employment Policy*) was being criticized because it did not categorically promise full employment, the government of the United States had nothing more concrete to offer than the slogans of its chief executive about '60 million jobs after the War'.

Yet it was to a favourable Administration that the workers must pin any hopes they had of a controlled transition to peace; and whether the war ended sooner or later than was guessed at in 1943, the head of that Administration would be chosen in 1944. Though he had no plans to put forward, Roosevelt had heretofore been as good as his word in defending labour's gains since 1933, and he would surely improvise something now. Official union policy must therefore be to blame the defects of his administration upon his lieutenants, and to accept whole-heartedly the task of mobilizing voters under the banner of a fourth term.

That task was in 1943 as urgent as it was formidable. In the previous year only 28m. of the 80m. citizens eligible to cast a ballot had done so – an alarming decline from almost 50m. in 1940 – and for the first time since 1930 Republican turn-out at the polls had actually exceeded Democratic. Some candidates, including the Chairman of the House Un-American Activities Committee, had been returned by about 5% of their con-stituents. This was government by default. Even more than in 1940, when the dozen largest American cities had given him his margin of victory, Roosevelt would need his urban plurali-ties in 1944. If the recent trend continued, no gain of the New Deal period could be considered safe.

To reverse the trend now required exceptional effort. A war-time President with the example of Wilson before him was inhibited from out-and-out appeals to the electorate in favour of his own party. Yet at ground level Democratic organizers found the task of keeping track of millions of migrant wartime voters, and particularly workers, virtually insuperable. Geo-graphical dispersal itself raised myriad problems of registration. Technical difficulties apart, labour strategists like Hillman were painfully aware of the mounting anti-union prejudices among a public exposed to slogans such as 'Our boys at the front are not working a forty-hour week'.

It was in these unpropitious circumstances that he and Murray devised a new pattern and reached a new pitch of political activity in order, as Murray explained to the CIO's 1943 national convention,

> to weld the unity of all workers, farmers and other progressives behind candidates . . . who support the war programme of our Commander-in-Chief and enlightened domestic and foreign policies; . . . to educate and unite the people of America and to present to them the tremendous issues at stake in the 1944 election

before propelling them to the polls in support of Roosevelt. The new machinery created for this purpose deserves close study because it has become the prototype for all subsequent political intervention by American unions. A 'Political Action Committee' of five men had been formed the previous July, 'to conduct a broad and intensive programme of education for the purpose of mobilizing the 5m. members of the CIO and enlisting the active support of all other trade unions, American Federation of Labour, Railroad Brotherhoods and unaffiliated, for effective labour action on the political front'. It immediately circularized all CIO unions urging them to establish their own Political Action Committees, where possible in co-operation with friendly non-labour groups, to cultivate intense activity before the next elections. Then for four weeks Hillman with top officials conducted a coast-to-coast mission to spread support for the new enterprise in a series of regional conferences, to test local reaction, learn of local problems, and elicit information upon which electoral strategy could be based. In New York Hillman had gathered together a headquarters staff – not all unionists, but all sharing a common New Deal background – and from there set up fourteen regional directorates responsible only to himself. By this small but talented cadre, covering the areas of organization, finance, legal counsel, Congressional liaison, publicity and propaganda, the new CIO-PAC's resources were marshalled, the initial strategy devised, and the opening fanfare of the 1944 campaign sounded.

Almost at once labour's new political arm attracted the attention of the special committees whereby Congress investigates electoral campaign expenditure. The House's special committee inspected PAC records and devoted eight of its twenty-one days of pre-election hearings to forty-four PAC witnesses from four cities. Their testimony gives a picture of Hillman's new organ and how it functioned in its first year of operations. At its New York headquarters were compiled the voting records and other details of candidates, which were transmitted through its regional directors to the state CIO bodies, in each of which a respective political action committee had been or was being formed. Without trying to influence the decisions of these bodies, each regional director was to contrive that their endorsements were collated and published simultaneously. Special PAC literature, now appearing in great quantity and high quality, followed the same path down from headquarters, and at state level was redistributed to union locals, each of which was urged to form its own corresponding political action committee to disseminate information and encourage its membership to register and to vote for PAC-endorsed candidates.

This new organization quickly became the target of hostile attacks from the right. Another Congressional body to accord it close interest was the House Un-American Activities Committee, whose chairman, the highly conservative Martin Dies, announced in January 1944 that the PAC was under investigation. Without taking oral evidence – for Hillman and his colleagues publicly challenged its competence in this field – the Dies Committee rushed into print with a report of more than two hundred pages, charging that at least one-third of the CIO's executive board 'followed the Communist line', that 'the political views and philosophy of the Communist Party and of the CIO-PAC coincide in every detail', and that the latter was conducting 'a subversive Communist campaign to subvert the Congress of the United States to its totalitarian programme'.

The scintilla of truth embedded in all this was the circumstance that Hillman's Clothing Workers were an important ingredient of the American Labour Party of New York, whose left wing comprised unions containing a number of Communists whose services he had not rebuffed but whom his union could not later shake off, and that their presence was to lead to the secession of the ALP's right wing to form the Liberal Party. When in November 1944 the ALP drew nearly 485,000 votes in the state which Roosevelt carried by only 300,000, the end might have appeared to justify the means. Nevertheless, this

7

local alliance with Communism made the CIO-PAC peculiarly vulnerable to witch-hunters.

A second charge it had to face, both in the Dies Committee and in the House Committee on Campaign Expenditures, was of attempting to coerce the rank-and-file unionist into political action for particular candidates against his own will. To the latter committee a PAC officer replied by protesting that

> the CIO-PAC is not a policy-making body. It is the political arm of the CIO . . . As such, we devote ourselves to carrying out the policies carefully formulated by the leaders of the CIO and endorsed by the rank and file of labour at a democratic convention of the CIO . . . For instance, the CIO goes on record as in favour of the 65-cent minimum hourly wage. That becomes part of our programme.

Towards the political action committees of state CIO bodies and of constituent CIO unions, the CIO-PAC

> simply act in an advisory capacity. If they want to take our advice they do so. If they ask us questions we will advise them, . . . and if they do not want to take our advice they go their own sweet way.

The PAC's national office, said Hillman, was there simply to co-ordinate

> the people who want to be co-ordinated. All we do is counsel with them and give them advice. We have no authority over them outside of giving our advice . . . For many years each of the affiliated unions of the CIO has conducted its own programme of political activity and political education. It is the function of our Committee to co-ordinate and make more effective the work which our constituent unions have heretofore carried on independently.

National CIO-PAC would stimulate registration campaigns, make available the voting records of Congressmen, and so forth, but was without power to compel lesser units to make use of these services or abide by the advice it proffered. Still less would it try to dictate any formal pattern of organization below the level of regional offices. Endorsement of candidates for political office was a matter for union bodies in the respective localities to decide, and their decisions were merely collated by the national office. Even the endorsement of Roosevelt himself was not treated as a foregone conclusion but deferred until May 1944, by when it had been made by the great majority of such units. In view of the regular transmission from headquarters of Congressmen's voting records, with the PAC's appraisals appended, the idea of a political blacklist has been abandoned with understandable reluctance by those who feel that the place of the union is outside politics. Nevertheless, the best answer to charges of political 'dictatorship', now as then, is the plain truth that no attempt to compel union members to uniformity of electoral behaviour can have the least certainty of success.

A third charge, that in pursuit of its un-American ends the CIO-PAC could dispose of 'huge slush funds', did not survive serious scrutiny. Nevertheless, legal constraint upon union political spending, of the kind to be looked at more closely in Chapter 6 below, was one of Hillman's reasons for going outside the CIO's thirty-nine constituent unions to canalize the support of progressive-minded groups and individuals in an auxiliary body called the National Citizens' Political Action Committee. At its peak in 1945 this lay adjunct claimed a membership of 18,000, among whom farmers, journalists and professional men and women predominated. But its financial support was less than expected, while its existence aroused misgivings about the centrifugal influence of 'intellectuals' on labour. At the end of 1946 the NC-PAC merged itself with the Progressive Citizens of America, and in 1948 went forward to the nomination of Henry Wallace for President, and extinction.

But by then the CIO-PAC had itself undergone change. At its 1944 national convention, on the morrow of Roosevelt's fourth victory, the CIO put it on a permanent footing and officially enumerated its duties thus:

a   To maintain and to stimulate the activities of existing
    political action committees, established in state and
    city industrial union councils and local unions, and to
    establish such bodies where they are not now organized.

b   To maintain, extend and stimulate the activity of
    community organizations formed under the leadership
    or with the participation of the CIO.

c To promote united action in the political field in collaboration with other organizations of labour, progressive groups, and forward-looking leaders of the two major political parties.

d To continue and intensify the work of securing the fullest possible exercise of the right of franchise by organization for a maximum registration and vote.

e To carry on the work of political education through the publication and distribution of pamphlets, servicing the labour press, the use of radio, and all other appropriate means.

f To perform the groundwork for effective participation in local elections of 1945 and in local, state and national elections in 1946.

Shortly thereafter the first step was taken towards integrating it more closely with the parent body by abolishing Hillman's regional offices and by channelling the PAC's main work through the CIO's own regional directors, internationals and locals. In May 1947, within a year of Hillman's death, the PAC's national executive board was reshaped to include a top officer from each of the CIO's largest unions, under Walter Reuther's chairmanship; and Hillman's post of director was filled by a former lieutenant of his in the Clothing Workers, Jack Kroll. A tactician and toiler where Hillman had been a strategist and visionary, Kroll had already been making the PAC organization in Ohio an exemplar for all other states. After the 1948 elections the national PAC moved into the CIO's Washington headquarters.

This absorption of the PAC within the institutional framework of the parent federation signified that political action had been incorporated into labour's normal routine, had been accepted as part of the annual rhythm of union business, where what was required for success was not an occasional blaze of publicity such as Hillman had ignited in 1943, but the slow-burning fuel to keep it going in campaign seasons and out. 'We are now committed,' said Murray in 1948,

> to developing and building our own independent ward, precinct and block organizations ... Intensive efforts are being made to establish permanent political action

committees within every local union, to be composed of
all officers, executive board members, shop stewards
and committeemen

and five years later he was able to report that such committees
had been

organized in virtually every state of the union and in every
industrial area of every state ... Particularly heartening
has been the number of union staff people detailed to full-
time political work.

The direction of political action in any unit was thus appor-
tioned somewhat loosely between the local CIO body and the
national PAC:

The PACs of the councils maintain contact with the PAC of
the national CIO. Nonetheless the state and local PACs
are regarded as committees of their respective councils, and
are responsible to those councils, subject to national PAC
policy.

National PAC's functions were to advise, stimulate and co-
ordinate. The intensity of local political action depended on
local circumstances, as did the shape of the local PAC itself.
But membership of the latter's officiate usually overlapped with
that of the parent CIO unit at each corresponding level,
fortified from time to time with the help of PAC fieldworkers
and organizers from Washington or from the state CIO-PAC.
The state CIO-PAC, because of its formal powers within the
CIO hierarchy, tended to be the controlling level for political
action also. With elections in view, many local PACs naturally
drew together to form Congressional district PACs for the
promotion and support of approved candidates. About such a
variety of formations, however, it is difficult to generalize.
Suffice it that some PAC units were shaped under pressure from
above, others sprang up from local roots.

No such an articulated system, of course, was at Hillman's
disposal in 1944. To that year we must briefly return, and ask
how effectively his new political creation performed in its first
campaign. 'The participation of labour in the political life of
the nation,' reported the Senate special committee on campaign

expenditures, 'was never more pronounced than it was in the election of 1944.' But the impact of the PAC, highly extemporary as its organization appeared, was bound to be uneven. It claimed first blood in the primaries when the abhorred Martin Dies announced his intention to withdraw after the PAC had helped raise registration in his Texan district 30% above any previous figure, and where (so Dies alleged) the CIO captured the Jefferson County Democratic convention. Two other members of his committee went down with him. But it is doubtful if Hillman had by November succeeded in organizing even half the states. Roosevelt, to be sure, ran somewhat more strongly than expected in the big cities whose large majorities carried their respective states for the Democrats; so that a cautious professional analyst of the returns, noting that organized workers had given Roosevelt 72% of their votes whereas non-union workers had given him only 56%, felt it safe to assert that

> union propaganda achieved the success at which it aimed. It succeeded in keeping alive the rising trend towards the New Deal in New York, in stopping the rising trend against the New Deal in the industrial states of the Middle West (except in Ohio) and of New England, and on the whole in restricting to the middle-class vote the trend away from Roosevelt.

'Nobody knows better than I do,' wrote Roosevelt to Hillman after it was over, 'how much you contributed to its success.' And even if in some areas the PAC's prestige was that of a rainmaker blessed by a cloudburst, the overall result, achieved in the third year of wartime dislocation, was gratifying to labour's new venture.

In one other important respect, too, Hillman was credited with a critical degree of influence. That was the choice of Roosevelt's running mate, which early in 1944 appeared to lie between Byrnes (unacceptable to labour) and Henry Wallace (incompatible with the party machine). Roosevelt's directive to 'Clear it with Sidney' may or may not have connoted, as was at the time believed, that PAC's chairman had won for labour something like a veto power over the composition of the Democratic ticket. But by the eve of the nominating convention,

Hillman according to his biographer had reached a clear understanding with Roosevelt that labour would do its best to persuade its friends in the Chicago convention hall not to block Truman.

So much – and much of that conjectural – for organized labour's influence on the choice of national politicians in the last American elections of World War II. We must finally consider what tangible results this electoral drive achieved with the return of peace. Out of months of planning and discussion had emerged from the CIO *The People's Programme for 1944*, and from its great rival *The Post-War Programme of the American Federation of Labour*. Both documents insisted that government must urgently concern itself not only with the traditional objectives of business unionism – higher wages and shorter hours – but also with the myriad varieties of ameliorative legislation which the New Deal had brought from the periphery to the centre of labour's attention – improved living and working standards; a full employment programme that would make it Washington's responsibility to maintain a high level of investment and spending; increased federal aid to education and housing; widening of social security, unemployment insurance and pension schemes; revision of the federal tax structure on the basis of 'ability to pay'; the fostering of equal racial opportunities in industry; and a strengthened Department of Labour. All these goals organized labour has been in political pursuit of ever since.

How did its quest fare in the immediately post-war years? So far as the Seventy-ninth and Eightieth Congresses went, very poorly. Nothing more clearly distinguishes the post-war political climate of the USA from that of Great Britain than the almost unqualified refusal of its legislature to respond to proposals for social reform, of which the pages of the *Congressional Record* from 1945 to 1948 are a veritable graveyard. By the latter year, in consequence, nearly half the country's working population remained excluded from any social security benefits, and the purchasing power of old-age beneficiaries had been reduced by inflation to below the 1935 level. The only significant measure adopted in the field of public housing was for veterans; in public health insurances for federal employees; in education, for school lunchers.

Against these many disappointments must be set one notable advance in the field of employment policy. While the United States Employment Service suffered decentralization, and the Department of Labour a cut in appropriations, a bill sponsored by Senator James E. Murray of Montana survived to reach the statute book. The so-called Employment Act of 1946, though falling short of its sponsor's desire for 'full' employment, and far short of *The CIO's Re-employment Plan* of 1945, nevertheless went some way to securing what President Truman called 'the right to work for every American citizen able and willing to work'.

The Murray Act made it the statutory responsibility of the federal government

to co-ordinate and utilize all its plans, functions and resources for the purpose of creating and maintaining, in a manner calculated to foster and promote free competitive enterprise and the general welfare, conditions under which there will be afforded useful employment opportunities, including self-employment, for those able, willing and seeking to work, and to promote maximum employment, production and purchasing power.

The President was required to submit to Congress at the beginning of every term an Economic Report, analysing the current situation and trends, reviewing his government's economic programme and making recommendations for carrying it out. This Report would be referred for continuing study to a newly created joint committee of Congress. In preparing it the President was to be assisted by a Council of not more than ten Economic Advisers within his Executive Office. Their products have come to cover an ever widening area of national policy in a skilful blend of diagnosis, practical advice and pious exhortation.

In retrospect the Employment Act of 1946 wears a double significance. It shows Congress laying upon the Administration the major duty of seeking to control the national economy through advance planning. Thus the Act gave formal recognition to what had been the informal though ineluctable trend of the dozen years preceding. It signifies also the displacement of one of labour's primary economic goals out of the purely industrial and into the primarily political arena, where hence-forward only political action could reach. This victory, the first important statute of post-war America, gave some satisfaction to the political leaders of her unions at a juncture when, as we shall see, every other battle on the Congressional front was going badly for them.

A note on union security

As union security under American collective bargaining agreements takes various forms, it may be convenient to distinguish them at this point.

The closed shop The employer agrees to employ none but members in good standing with their union. Since 1 April 1959, such agreements have been illegal in interstate commerce: but some exist in certain sections of the construction industry.

The union shop The most widespread form of security clause, though many variants of it exist. All present employees, and all hired thereafter, shall for the duration of the agreement remain union members in good standing after a preliminary thirty-day period. An employee, however, need only offer to pay the regular dues of the union in order to avoid discharge: his expulsion from the union for any reason other than refusal to pay dues cannot of itself constitute grounds for discharge.

Maintenance of membership A compromise used chiefly during World War II. All present members of the union, and all who thereafter become members, must as a condition of employment retain their union membership for the duration of the agreement.

The agency shop A comparatively recent form of union security. Present employees who are not and do not wish to become union members shall, as a condition of employment, pay to the union each month a service charge equal to the amount of the regular monthly dues. This is in consideration of the fact that under the Taft-Hartley Act a certified union must represent (and therefore service) *all* employees in that bargaining unit.

5

The conservatism of
Senator Taft

The post-war period of turbulence, of strikes and rising prices, was needless to say desired by neither labour, management nor government. All three made deliberate efforts to avert it. In March 1945 three labour leaders sat down with three representatives of the US Chamber of Commerce to agree that 'free competition and free men are the strength of our free society', with labour acknowledging 'the inherent right and responsibility of management to direct the operations of an enterprise', and management recognizing labour's right to organize and bargain collectively. But the sudden ending of the war with Japan meant a more rapid return to normalcy than either side was then anticipating. In October began the dismantling of all wage controls which were not expected directly to influence prices, and just as abruptly collective bargaining was restored.

A small tripartite conference of business, union and public representatives, summoned to Washington by the new President in the following month, sat for three weeks to no great purpose. The unions were demanding an overdue increase in basic wage rates, to be met out of profits and productivity. The employers retorted that these profits would be absorbed by the costs of reconversion and that the prerequisite for sustained productivity in peacetime was the removal of price controls. After this failure each participant went its own way. President Truman invited Congress to enact 'well-reasoned and workable legislation' to meet the proximate threat of industrial unrest: labour resorted to direct action: management withdrew to close its ranks. When the three separate trails converged again it was at the passage of the Taft-Hartley Act eighteen months later.

During 1946 Congress first diminished and then destroyed the Office of Price Administration, at a time when a backlog of deferred consumer demand was being let loose on a market where essential commodities were still in short supply; and the consumer price index rocketed up. This nullified the effect of a first round of strikes which by February had already lost the country more man-hours than the whole of 1943 and 1944 combined. Its course entailed a General Motors strike of 113 days, further governmental seizures of mines and railroads, upheld by 5 to 4 in the Supreme Court, and Truman's appearance before a joint session of Congress to seek emergency strike-breaking powers. The mid-term elections of 1946, by when a second round of wage demands was in sight, marked labour's worst electoral setback since Hoover's day. The CIO was no more than frank in describing it as 'a signal defeat for the liberal and labour voters of America'. Barely 38% of the potential electorate balloted. Hillman, architect of so many labour-liberal alliances, had died four months earlier. Only 73 out of the PAC's 318 endorsees were returned to the House, only 5 out of 21 to the Senate. Defeats were incurred in the very heartlands of unionism such as Detroit.

On 3 January 1947 a Republican Congress assembled in Washington with the air of men who had at long last succeeded in bringing under control a fire that had raged for fourteen years. It is hard to accept at face value the cries of angry astonishment raised by labour leaders when amendment of the Wagner Act became a reality, for the counter-attack had long been preparing. Congressional pressure upon the National Labour Relations Board had secured a rightward shift not only in its personnel but also in its interpretations – a shift which Taft-Hartley was formally to recognize. By the time that Act came into force some thirty-four states had already enacted their own laws to restrict in one way and another the unions' freedom to strike or picket, to secure closed shop agreements or to conduct their own internal affairs without public supervision. Most of these laws the federal courts had refused to invalidate, and between them they contained almost every ingredient stirred into the federal statute. Over Capitol Hill itself the storm signals were flying. Before the Seventy-Ninth Congress lay some eighty bills to circumscribe various union practices deemed contrary to public policy; legislators' blood-pressure had just been raised by the stormiest year in the history of American industrial relations; and further big strikes were pending.

In view of such clear notices of intent from Congress, from the states and from the Administration (whose milder proposals Congress brushed aside), it is almost incredible that labour should have continued to gamble on the chance that no drastic legislation would ensue. Yet its behaviour is inexplicable upon any other supposition. Instead of recognizing the urgent need to compromise and bring forward counter-proposals of its own, the small pro-labour bloc in Congress contented itself with voting blankly against all bills to regulate union activity in any degree whatsoever. This was of no help to the larger number of moderates who urged a cautious and piecemeal approach, after due investigation. Rather it enabled the coalition of agrarian Republicans and southern Democrats to ride down all middle-of-the-road proposals with tougher ones; towards which the pro-labour groups thereupon adopted a policy of passive resistance, seemingly confident that the more extreme the measure passed by the House, the smaller its chances of clearing the Senate. Indeed it appeared that labour lobbyists repeatedly tried to stimulate House action on restrictive bills, in the belief that the larger liberal block in the Senate would be happier if given something to get its teeth into. As soon as control of Congress passed from the President's party to its opponents, the odds against this gamble succeeding lengthened considerably.

Without delay the new Senate and House labour committees commenced hearings which were to occupy more than six weeks and over 8,000 pages. Two versions of an omnibus bill had passed the respective houses by 13 May. To the measure agreed in conference committee Truman on 20 June applied his veto, which within three days had been overridden. Although his message declared that the bill 'violates principles essential to our public welfare', 'raises serious issues of public policy', 'would go far towards destroying our national unity', and 'is a clear threat to the successful workings of our democratic society', yet in neither House had Administration spokesmen rallied the party against it.

The measure of 1947, surviving with few amendments today, is an exhaustive one. Unlike the Wagner Act, whose twelve pages reappeared with significant changes as Title I, the Taft-Hartley, nearly three times as long, goes outside the sphere of collective bargaining in its endeavour to encompass the labour-management relationship in its entirety. President Truman had proposed that reform should be piecemeal: Congress had taken one huge bite. A complete federal labour code, the first of its kind, was thereby compressed into a single statute, or more precisely into the first three of its five titles, whose complexity of content has been likened to a set of interlocking railway time-tables or an intricate corporation mortgage designed to cover every eventuality. The President had asked that extensive in-quiry should precede legislation: Congress subscribed to a belief in action first, investigation afterwards. Title IV created a Congressional joint committee to study the problems which the rest of the Act purported to solve, and to make a final report not later than January 1949.

One major assumption of the Act's co-sponsors was that the power of organized labour had become overweighted with respect to management's. The Wagner Act, they argued, had probably increased the number of industrial disturbances in-directly by increasing labour's corporate strength and so emboldening it to 'take on' management oftener than formerly. At the passage of the Wagner bill union membership was between 3m. and 4m., mostly in trades or crafts: now it stood at nearly 17m. and covered most of the basic industries. It seemed a fair assumption that whatever protection and encouragement the unions might have required in 1935 they needed now no longer. The plain duty of legislators was therefore to remove the statutory bias which they and the public believed to have been imparted to industrial relations twelve years earlier, so as to restore equality of bargaining power between the two sides. Against the group of five 'unfair labour practices' of employers, herein reproduced, the new Act accordingly set a greater number of unfair practices of labour unions, some of which went outside the collective bargaining procedure itself. Thus, the union might not refuse to bargain collectively with the employer in good faith, might not engage in secondary or 'hot goods' boycotts, jurisdictional strikes or restrictive practices (including 'feather-bedding'). Whether picketing also was restricted would depend on how the courts interpreted 'coercion' of an employer, which was forbidden the union in certain circumstances. A union's freedom to strike without notice was qualified, and a strike by government employees absolutely forbidden.

Such restrictions appeared in labour's eyes to imply notions about the very nature of workers' co-operation which antedated contemporary industrial conditions by many decades – that the only men interested in a dispute with a particular employer are his own hands; that a union is not part of a movement in which each tries to assist the growth and effectiveness of all, but a mere aggregation of individual workers. The employer's position, on the other hand, was somewhat eased. He was at all times to be free to put his own point of view before his men, short of using 'threat of reprisal or force or promise of benefit'. His lower supervisory staff were in various ways discouraged from unionization. He need not bargain on a basis broader than a single plant. His contributing to a union trust fund – whose purposes and administration the Act specified in some detail – was made conditional upon his written contractual agreement, and he was to enjoy his full share of control over the fund.

A second assumption of the framers was that the excessive power enjoyed by unions was inimical to public policy generally, because conducive to activities which impaired the free flow of commerce. Accordingly, the government was now empowered to seek an injunction placing an eighty-day moratorium on any dispute which would in the President's opinion 'if permitted to continue, imperil the nation's health or safety'. This requirement, empowering the President to order a temporary resumption of work, has proved unconducive to settlements, and three successive Presidents (including Mr Nixon) have asked Congress, so far in vain, for more flexible alternatives. In ordinary disputes, too, the NLRB was required to give prior attention to those where an employer could reasonably allege that 'substantial or irreparable injury' might be occasioned him by certain

unfair practices (secondary and hot goods boycotts and jurisdictional strikes), and to move the courts. The latter were in
turn required to enjoin the union concerned and to proceed to a
decision on the merits if the dispute were not settled within
ten days thereafter. Another section declared the above-men-
tioned labour practices to be not only unfair but illegal; and
'whosoever shall be injured in his business or property' – a
potentially enormous category – by such practices, was permitted to sue the union for damages and costs. This, when
taken together with the Act's reaffirmation that any union
could 'sue or be sued as an entity . . . in the courts of the
United States', encouraged the further inference that a union
was corporately responsible for any and all acts performed by
its members or agents.

Union security was to be limited to the union shop agreement,
with the proviso that at least 30% of the employees desired it.
Craft workers might have separate representation if they chose.
Where certification of the bargaining unit was sought, the
NLRB was to conduct a secret ballot from which strikers not
entitled to reinstatement would be excluded. After four years'
experience, during which workers had voted the union shop in
over 90% of the elections held by the Board, Congress repealed
this provision as wasteful of time and money. The need was emphasized for continuing governmental scrutiny of the certified
union's internal affairs. None might enjoy the services or protection of the Board that had not provided the Secretary of
Labour, and its own membership, with an extensive and up-to-
date report, containing a detailed financial statement and
copies of its constitution and by-laws. In addition all its officers
were required to file an affidavit, executed within the last twelve
months, of non-association with the Communist party. Though
it requires no similar affirmation from employers, the Supreme
Court has upheld this provision. Only the Mineworkers have
been strong and monopolistic enough to be able to dispense
with the NLRB's services. Their refusal to file was the cause of
their once again disaffiliating from the AFL, in December
1967.

A third assumption was that the power of organized labour
menaced also the individual worker, who must, therefore, be
protected against coercion, whether used directly by his union

or by his employer at the union's behest. Several of the new 'unfair labour practices' were accordingly designed to give him practical assurance of the rights formally guaranteed. He was not to be forced to join a union against his will. While the union might continue to make whatever conditions of membership it pleased, where the NLRB deemed these conditions discriminatory it would refuse certification. No certified union might procure the discharge of any worker from his job for any reason save failure to pay his dues or an initiation fee of reasonable size. Again, the individual employee might present a grievance to his employer directly, without routing it through the shop steward and setting in motion the normal grievance machinery. The check-off of his dues was no longer to be automatic but conditional upon his own periodic and written authorization. Where federal conciliators were active, his union might not call him out on strike before the employer's final offer had been submitted for his approval or rejection by secret ballot. Such restrictions were obnoxious to labour leaders, as assuming without question that a union's officiate, so far from being the servant of the rank and file, is frequently unresponsive to the latter's 'real' needs, or almost of the nature of 'outside bosses' with whom management must continually compete for the worker's allegiance; and that if there were no coercion members would repudiate their union or be weaned away from it by individual consideration from the employer.

In several ways the Act also strove to bind government in the labour field to a position of greater detachment. For instance, it transferred all functions, records and personnel of the Labour Department's Conciliation Service (where ex-unionists were plentiful) to a new and independent agency, the Federal Mediation and Conciliation Service. An independent General Counsel, too, was created to supervise the personnel and activities of an enlarged NLRB. Labour's freedom to influence government electorally, by expenditures on political campaigning, was restricted by means and to an extent which will require separate notice (p. 151 below).

Most repugnant of all to the unions was the Act's Section 14(b), providing that in the matter of union security its provisions were to yield to state law wherever the latter was the more stringent. In effect, where state laws prohibited even a watered-down version of the union shop, they were to prevail over the qualified permission of the federal statute.

On labour's bitter and voluble indignation over passage of the 'slave labour Act' we need not dwell longer than is necessary to explain the reasons for it. If the Act's promoters represented its purpose to be the correction of abuses which had arisen since the Wagner Act, to union leaders it appeared in some respects to be going farther back than this. Its union shop provisions, for one thing, ignored closed shop traditions which in some industries went back half a century. That state enactments in this field were, where stricter, to be given precedence over federal looked like a return to the bad old American view that an economic problem is better thrashed out 48 times than once, or at least a denial that the problem of union organization was strictly a national one at all. More alarming was the apparent revival of doctrines and procedures which since the Norris-La Guardia Act had been thought obsolete – that the proper place for the settlement of a labour dispute was the courtroom and an injunction on the employer's behalf a proper way to get it there. No corresponding remedy was provided for the union faced with unfair practice by the employer. Nothing in the new law prevented the employer from securing the co-operation of fellow employers to break a strike, whereas the union might not seek the help of other unions to make it effective. Even where resort was not had to an injunction, pre-strike and post-strike plebiscites could slow down the union's activity to a full stop. As for the return to damage suits, this seemed to lay the union wide open to liability for acts (including unauthorized acts) of its members, while its officiate was simultaneously deprived of any real control (beyond expulsion for non-payment of dues) over their conduct.

One prediction at least about the consequences of Taft-Hartley was at once fulfilled. In his veto message Truman had warned that 'by raising barriers between labour and management and by injecting political considerations into normally economic decisions' the Act 'would invite the workers to gain their ends through direct political action'. Immediately after its passage the AFL's executive council met to plan the defeat of every member of Congress who voted for its final enactment. At the following national convention the AFL unanimously

8

accepted the council's proposals for establishing a new organ, later called Labour's League for Political Education (LLPE). In structure, terms of reference and means of financial support the new League was a clear, though unacknowledged, imitation of the CIO-PAC. Its national committee of about thirty members were almost all presidents of constituent AFL unions, its chairman and secretary being those of the parent Federation. Its director was Joseph Keenan, one of Hillman's wartime assistants on the National Defence Advisory Committee. All state federations and central labour bodies were urged to establish organs of political action at their respective levels in time for the 1948 campaigns. Like CIO-PAC, the League and local political committees were to seek to co-operate with all likeminded groups. Politically, the AFL had swung into line with the CIO, representatives of League and PAC henceforward appearing frequently and officially together on the same platforms in cordial liaison. Joint political committees were being formed in many localities. To that extent labour had closed its ranks; and united, as its leaders claimed, 'went to the polls as never before' on behalf of a Democratic party which had adopted virtually the whole labour platform with repeal of Taft-Hartley at the top of the list.

Electoral results in November augured well. The new LLPE reckoned 172 endorsees sent to Washington and claimed that 'not one single Senator who voted against the Taft-Hartley law was defeated and not one single friendly seat in the House of Representatives was lost'. 'We used our votes,' said Murray for the CIO, 'we used them well': and the *CIO News* was jubilant that '120 T-H.ers Won't Be Back'. State and municipal contests had gone equally well – in labour's eyes repeal had been given a clear popular mandate.

But the biggest surprise of all, for labour as well as for the press and the professionals, was Truman's victory over Dewey by little more than 2m. ballots. This despite the Progressive Party candidature of Henry A. Wallace, which had attracted the unofficial support of fifteen unions representing some 11% of the CIO's membership and come near to splitting its executive board. The main effects of Wallace's intervention were to fracture the American Labour Party of New York and give that state to Dewey. But did labour really get out the vote for

Truman? The total poll was just about the 1944 level: unionists, and railroad unionists particularly, were believed to bulk large among abstainers. LLPE's spot checks indicated only 35% of AFL membership to be in units possessing some kind of political action committee, and only about half of these to have polled. Six highly industrialized states swung out of the Democratic column, and in three others the Truman lead was minute. Commentators were fairly agreed that the President owed his overall lead to compensatory gains in the mid-west. A generally accepted inference, on the other hand, was that in the big cities the lower-income groups had turned out in greater strength for the Democrats than in 1944.

Be that as it may, the President asked the Eighty-First Congress for outright repeal of Taft-Hartley, and submitted a newly-written substitute which the legislature proceeded to consider side by side with other proposals. Whether because of the welter of alternatives, or because of Truman's barefisted approach, or because of inept floor leadership in the Senate against Taft's skilful parliamentary management, or because of the residual strength of the conservative coalition – for one or more of these reasons labour's lobbyists were left to calculate that in the crucial vote they were short of five supporters in the Senate and fourteen in the House. The opportunity passed and has never since recurred. Though unionism has never ceased to demand repeal, or at least wholesale amendment, public opinion subsided rapidly into indifference as to the rights and wrongs of the Act, and workers themselves when polled in 1950 did not seem markedly more antagonistic than the public at large. The mid-term elections, while leaving Democrats in control of the two Houses, so weakened the liberal wings in both as to make resumption of the repeal campaign unpromising. The year brought one further ignominy for labour. For the attack on Senator Robert A. Taft the two great federations threw into Ohio over $1m. and their best political organizers and publicists. Yet not only was Taft returned by an increased plurality, but his lead was piled up chiefly in those industrial areas of the state where unionism was strong.

In other ways beside failure to repeal Taft-Hartley, the 'Eighty-Worst' Congress (as Truman called it) had not lived up to liberals' expectations. Labour was gratified with a housing act and a raising of the statutory minimum wage, but mourned the death of bills to widen aid to education and to institute compulsory national health insurance. The run-down of the Labour Department was halted. The Social Security Act of 1935 was amended to cover another 10m. citizens, and to nearly double their monthly benefits under Old Age and Survivors Insurance (OASI). But 14m. workers, mostly agricultural, remained outside the scheme; and a bill to broaden the coverage of unemployment insurance failed.

Immediately after Taft-Hartley, labour's caution about how it would be applied led to a brief lull in strikes. During the mild recession of 1949–50, however, a fifth round of post-war wage increases took place. Of new contracts, that between Auto Workers and General Motors, to run for five years, was justly regarded as the New Model, containing as it did a built-in annual wage 'improvement factor' of $2\frac{1}{2}\%$ in return for a virtual guarantee of uninterrupted production. That same year of 1950, however, saw the outbreak of the Korean War, which was markedly to change the nation's economic and political climate. Unionism's prompt request that the government adopt sweeping economic controls was only partially met by a Defence Production Act allowing a supervision of wages and prices too limited to check the swift inflationary trend. A spate of 'beat-the-freeze' wage demands was one reason for the AFL and CIO's significant decision in 1951 to combine their pressures upon government through a single United Labour Policy Committee which embraced also the Railroad Brotherhoods and the Machinists. Truman responded by giving both federations representation on a new National Advisory Board and a resuscitated Wage Stabilization Board. It was not enough to forestall a railway strike necessitating the moving-in of the Army to run the railroads, or to prevent the development of the steel strike of 1952, where the President's seizure of the mills was ruled unconstitutional in a celebrated Supreme Court case.

Engagement in the Far East, following as it did upon the Cold War, generated also a widespread feeling of frustration and insecurity which found partial relief in the type of anti-Communist campaign typified by Senator Joe McCarthy. This, while focusing chiefly on the executive branch of government and the incumbent Democrats, did not ignore trade unions. One

boon of Wallace's failure in 1948 was the opportunity it gave
the national CIO to apply discipline to its Communists, that
embarrassing legacy from its organizing years, by now estimated to number about 30,000 but including a high proportion
of officers. Its 1949 convention witnessed the expulsion of the
Electrical Workers (UEW) and the Farm Equipment Workers,
and the amendment of its constitution so as to expel and dis-
qualify from membership of the national executive committee
any member or active supporter of a totalitarian party. Thus
empowered, and after lengthy hearings, a subcommittee of the
board had by August 1950 revoked the charters of nine more
internationals and gone far to recover their membership by
readmission into new and reformed units. This self-purgation
made easier both co-operation with the AFL and compliance
with the affidavit requirements of Taft-Hartley. It did not avail,
however, to allay public anxiety about the internal affairs of
unions.

With the 1952 elections in view, labour tuned up its political
machines to support candidates favouring a strong anti-inflation
programme and accelerated social legislation, and opposing
Taft-Hartley. Upon this last score, labour's tactics during the
Eighty-Second Congress had been shifting away from insistence
on outright repeal and towards limited amendments, among
which individual unions unhappily differed as to the desirable
priority. Both the Democratic platform and its Presidential
candidate condemned the statute unequivocally. Nevertheless
the labour federations withheld their endorsement of Stevenson
until – an occasion without precedent – both he and Eisenhower
had addressed their national conventions. Analysis of the election returns led to the conclusion that, while the rest of the
nation was going 3 to 2 for Eisenhower, union members voted
in the same ratio for Stevenson; but that their families slipped
away from their normal Democratic allegiance by balloting 9
to 8 for the General.

The Republican candidate's overwhelming victory at the
polls was not the only personal factor marking a change in
labour's relations with government. Within a few weeks death
removed the aged heads of both federations. Green was succeeded in the AFL by the blunt and belligerent, though essentially conservative, George Meany. The place of Philip Murray,

so long the patient victim of Lewis's taunts, was filled by a forty-five-year-old man of distinctly positive and progressive outlook, Walter P. Reuther, former Socialist and head of the Automobile Workers.

In his first message the new President handed over to Congress the consideration of some limited amendments to Taft-Hartley. Ironically, Taft's own death in July 1953 diminished the chance of any changes that would not be more stringent. Labour was placed on the defensive; the one unionist in the President's cabinet resigned the Secretaryship of Labour in despair; and in the following session union lobbyists narrowly headed off an Administration measure which would have made all strikes conditional upon an NLRB-sponsored poll of union membership. Meanwhile the Korean War was indeed brought to an end: but steps to take up the slack in defence production were so small as to leave at the end of 1954 about 3¼m. unemployed and some 8m. employed only part-time. True, unemployment insurance and OASI coverage were extended. But while oil interests throve and higher incomes attracted greater tax relief, appropriations for the Labour Department were cut and nothing further was done for poorer citizens in the fields of housing and education. Twenty million and more workers still remained outside the protection of the Fair Labour Standards Act. Renewed electoral efforts by labour at mid-term helped slightly to increase the Democrats' strength in the Senate and to recapture control of the House: whereafter Congress raised the minimum wage to a dollar an hour. A number of states improved their social benefits, and further state inroads upon union security were in most cases successfully resisted. Labour-management relations were on the whole quiet; and something like a milestone was reached when in June 1955 several unions, headed by the Auto Workers, secured contracts containing an element of 'guaranteed' wage for workers unemployed up to six months.

Behind the scenes, however, AFL and CIO were busy arranging to reunite. Discussions to this end, abortively entered into after the Republicans' Congressional victory of 1947, had been renewed after their capture of the White House in 1952 and the demise of the two veteran labour presidents. *Rapprochement* now proceeded by way of a no-raiding pact between the bodies, ratified in their respective conventions, and the drafting by a Unity Committee of a new constitutional instrument to provide a single mode of governance for a body which should impartially embrace both craft- and industrial-type unions while preserving the structural autonomy of each. In the closing days of 1955 the two federations voted successively and almost unanimously to re-merge as the AFL-CIO.

At state and city levels, reunification was to move at a snail's pace for several years more. But at national level labour's two political arms (PAC and LLPE) flowed swiftly together into a single Committee on Political Education (COPE). Under the joint directorship of Kroll and McDevitt, this new organ proceeded at once to inject new enthusiasm and vigour into the campaign preparations of 1956, holding a series of regional conferences to activate the latent unionist vote on a nation-wide scale in November. If their efforts did not suffice to deflect an Eisenhower victory greater than the last, they at least helped secure substantial Democratic gains in Congress, which during his second term improved and widened social legislation of the New Deal era and enacted two salary increases for 1½m. federal employees, the second over the President's veto. In the states, too, where many labour-supported candidates had gained Assembly seats and governors' mansions, social benefits were markedly enlarged.

Economic recession in 1957–8 proved an electoral bogey for the party of Hoover. The Democratic tide, however, though flowing even more strongly at the midterm, did not carry into the statute book more than one additional piece of significant social legislation – a limited voluntary programme of medical care for the aged – or amend Taft-Hartley even to the limited extent envisaged by the Secretary of Labour, James P. Mitchell, when he addressed the AFL-CIO's 1958 national convention. Indeed, there was a large irony in the circumstance that the Eighty-Sixth Congress, ostensibly the most liberal and pro-labour in twenty years, should turn out to be the agent for extending further the Act's restrictions upon the internal affairs of trade unions. But such was the consequence of the findings of a Senate special committee to investigate Improper Activities in the Labour or Management Field.

The background of this committee's inquiry, chaired by

Senator McClellan, requires some understanding of 'ethical' and 'un-ethical' union practices. In January 1953 the AFL, faced with evidence of large-scale exploitation and extortion by its Longshoremen's international (ILA) on the New York and New Jersey waterfronts, had delivered it an unprecedented ultimatum. Either the union must remove all corrupt national and local officers and all representatives with criminal records, and establish democratic internal practices and fair hiring procedures, or else it would face expulsion. Refusal of the ILA to comply led to the withdrawal of its charter, and to three years of turbulence before the AFL had regathered most of the ex-communicated brothers under the wing of a newly-chartered body, the International Brotherhood of Longshoremen. With this a reformed and readmitted ILA was merged in 1959. In the meantime the AFL had overhauled its auditing system, and both it and the CIO adopted codes of ethical practices in the administration of union health and welfare funds. After re-merger the AFL-CIO scrutinized the nefarious officiate of the Teamsters Union and expelled that union, about 1½m. strong, together with two smaller unions, in 1957. It also purged the Textile Workers.

The McClellan committee, however, uncovered in its first report of March 1958 so much evidence of union racketeering, crime and violence, particularly in the Teamsters, as to cause the American public severe shock and the entire labour move-ment, most of which was blameless, serious embarrassment. Court proceedings were subsequently commenced against the Teamsters' new president (James R. Hoffa) and his predecessor (Dave Beck); the one on charges of having accepted the kind of payments from employers forbidden by Taft-Hartley, the other for having allegedly embezzled union funds and filed false tax returns. But it became clear to legislators that neither criminal prosecution of union officers nor undertakings by labour to set its own house in order would appease public indignation. If statutory control were not in some degree introduced, and promptly, the Democratic party would be in trouble in 1960. Senator John Kennedy (whose brother Robert was the Mc-Clellan committee's chief counsel) therefore co-sponsored a bill including AFL-CIO-favoured provisions to combat abuses in the handling of union funds. This cleared the Senate but did not get a majority when brought to the floor of the House, despite a telegram from Meany to every Congressman. A labour-supported Welfare and Pensions Plan Disclosure Act, however, did reach the statute book that year. Relevant bills in the following session included the much tougher Landrum-Griffin measure. The AFL-CIO, some of whose constituent unions were at cross purposes, once again repeated its miscalculations of 1947 by adopting an all-or-nothing strategy, rigidly refusing to compromise and accept the only milder alternative that had a chance of enactment. Lobbying by the Teamsters themselves was particularly inept. Eisenhower, greatly influenced by business lobbies, threw his weight behind Landrum-Griffin in a very one-sided speech broadcast from coast to coast, to which the Speaker of the House was given inadequate opportunity to reply. Mail from constituents increasingly demanded a statute with teeth: what finally emerged from a conference commit-tee of both Houses, to be signed by the President on 14 September 1959, did not lack them.

The Labour-Management Reporting and Disclosure Act, loosely called the Landrum-Griffin Act, is three-pronged. First, it amended Taft-Hartley with, on the whole, added stringency. Unions (a few industries excepted) might no longer negotiate clauses with management allowing them to refuse to handle 'hot cargo' (i.e., 'blacked' goods) – agreements wherein much of the Teamsters' strength had hitherto resided. 'Organizational' picketing, that is, picketing designed to force an employer to recognize a particular union without his employees' consent, was limited to thirty days. Secondly, the Act sought to eliminate certain administrative abuses, particularly in the handling by officers of a trade union's often very considerable funds. All unions are required to file a detailed financial statement annu-ally, and their officials must declare any personal financial interests which might conflict with union policy. No union might employ in its affairs any person who in the preceding five years had been convicted of a criminal offence or (until the Supreme Court in 1965 voided the provision as 'a bill of attainder') a member of the Communist party. Thirdly, the Act of 1959 makes provisions governing union election pro-cedures and protecting the equal rights of individual members to participate in them, as voters or candidates. A union must elect, by direct and secret ballot, its national officers at least twice every five years and its local officers every three years. Any aggrieved member may make a confidential complaint to the Secretary of Labour, who may investigate and, if he sees fit, move a federal court to order a new election.

From even this summary account it will be clear that Landrum-Griffin had very well-founded *raison d'être* in the behaviour of a minority of unions; that in certain respects it carries further the trend of Taft-Hartley towards greater governmental regulation of union affairs; and that in so doing it greatly extends the power of the Secretary of Labour in particular, as well as of the courts. For the underlying rationale of the Act was that, since public law countenances unions and makes membership of them virtually compulsory upon the worker, government must on the latter's behalf ensure that they are conducted in a manner compatible with their protected status.

It was also apparent that labour had misread the signs of the Democrats' mid-term gains. Evidently it did not possess influence enough to carry the Congress on an issue where it stood alone and at odds with moderate legislators. Disappointment in unionism's ranks – all the greater in view of its recently enhanced political activity – was vented when in the following year it opposed giving the Democratic Presidential nomination to Lyndon Johnson, who as Senate majority leader was believed to have acquiesced too readily in Landrum-Griffin's passage. Other probable consequences we may note in passing: that the statute has put larger unions in a better position than small to give the professional scrutiny and servicing which intricate federal regulation now requires; and that the increasing dependence on every union's national headquarters for such service may well have led to a decline in local autonomy. Certainly the Act has not perceptibly reduced either the Teamsters' hold over American transportation or the funds available for the legal defence of its ebullient leader, who was not put behind bars until five more years had elapsed. Labour's unfavourable image generally, on the other hand, was an undoubted handicap to its organizing drives of 1959 and 1960 which a public relations programme costing the AFL-CIO $1·2m. did not remove.

Deep discontent with the fruits, both political and economic, of the Eisenhower years led most labour delegates at the 1960 Democratic convention to vote to endorse Kennedy, attracted particularly by his professed intention to pit the powers of the federal government against economic stagnation. Unemployment was then standing at about 5m. The Republican platform proposed that unions should be made unambiguously subject to anti-trust laws. Kennedy's wafer-thin popular majority over Nixon undoubtedly owed something to labour votes in the metropolitan areas of industrialized states, all of which, save Ohio and California, he carried, though often by very narrow margins. From the AFL-CIO's more than usually extensive programme for the stimulation of economic regrowth, the new President drew items for his own. Congress responded by appropriating hundreds of millions of dollars for public works, for distressed areas and urban renewal, mainly through an expanded housing scheme and an Area Redevelopment Act of 1961. By the Manpower Development and Training Act of the following session Congress both encouraged and rewarded the acquisition of skilled labour qualifications. The minimum wage was raised to $1·25 an hour and extended to cover another 3·6m. workers, including for the first time employees in the hotel, restaurant and laundry trades. Congress raised the salaries of federal employees also, whose right to organize was now recognized by Presidential executive order. Social security was enhanced by further extending benefits to the retired, the unemployed and their dependent children. Labour-supported measures in the fields of education and hospital care, however, did not similarly thrive. After 1962, moreover, when at one point unemployment touched 4½m., the Administration shifted its main efforts for economic growth towards the restimulation of purchasing power through tax reform and reduction, in which it did not so consistently see eye to eye with organized labour.

Nor was labour entirely satisfied with the new Kennedy approach to the problems of collective bargaining. In an effort to obtain wider consensus, the President remitted this thorny topic to a specially created and tripartite Advisory Committee on Labour-Management Relations, where the public was represented, as part of a wide-ranging analysis of the prerequisites for national prosperity in the 1960s. The Committee duly recommended major changes in labour-management legislation;

especially means for prompter and more effective Presidential intervention in strikes requiring emergency treatment, including power to recommend conditions for settlement. Meanwhile the government's concern with 'the public interest' in collective bargaining was emphasized by the frequency with which the Secretary of Labour, Mr Arthur J. Goldberg, the energetic ex-General Counsel of the AFL-CIO, intervened in industrial disputes of all kinds. Some pro-labour bias was detectable in Kennedy's publicly castigating steel companies for 'ruthless disregard of their public responsibility' in proposing to raise prices, while he failed to rebuke Reuther's loudly professed intention to secure 'catch-up raises' for missile workers. So unionism muted its demands for a shorter working week and co-operated; though not without grumbling and some attempts to kick holes in the Administration's policy of trying to limit wage rises to increases in the rate of current national economic growth. Few disputes of that time were so long and inconclusively protracted as that over changes in railroad services and personnel, still raging after Kennedy's term of office was ended by the assassin's bullet in November 1963.

The Goldwater threat galvanized labour as never before. Expenditure on 'political education' rose steeply. In the electoral campaign of 1964, COPE and the political organs of other labour groups conducted drives of unparalleled intensity to get their members registered and to the polls on behalf of friendly candidates. Precise estimate of its success was made difficult by the very magnitude of Johnson's triumph. But COPE claimed victory for 25 of its 31 endorsees for the Senate, 234 of its 351 for the House: and in the Eighty-Ninth Congress labour reckoned 60 'friends' in the upper chamber and 248 in the lower. Many of the labour-backed proposals consequently brought to fruition, whether or not as part of the 'Great Society' to which the AFL-CIO convention gave its approval, were those that had been balked in Congress under Johnson's predecessor. A Department of Housing and Urban Affairs was created, with a Negro as its first Secretary. The 'anti-poverty' legislation, designed to help the under-skilled especially, was implemented swiftly and with particular attention to the 360 distressed counties of the Appalachian region. The poor of such rural areas and of the cities were to be beneficiaries also of a large-scale measure of aid for public education, to provide without delay more buildings, teachers, libraries and equipment. Above all, the new Congress enacted the long-desired medicare legislation to move the aged, and other Americans willing to take out low-cost health insurance, off public assistance and on to social security rolls. By 1968, too, unemployment in the country's civilian labour force had dropped markedly to a 3·6% average: even then, however, about one unemployed worker in five exhausted his benefits before finding work.

Though the Ninetieth Congress, elected at mid-term, contained markedly fewer members of liberal leanings, the spring of social reform did not dry up. With the mounting cost of the Vietnam war, however, and pressure from President Johnson for a tax increase, the rate of flow was somewhat diminished in a Congress looking for ways to hold down domestic governmental spending. The major legislative item of 1968 was the largest-ever increase in the social insurance system, bringing higher benefits to 24m. citizens, particularly to the disabled, widows and retired persons. These changes, Johnson noted, would lift another million Americans above the official poverty line; and, combined with the amendments of 1965, signified a rise of 23% in cash payments under the social security programme during his Presidency. In addition he appointed a Commission on Income Maintenance; his War on Poverty programmes escaped intact; money was voted for the Administration's 'model cities' programme to combat urban evils; and federal aid to elementary and secondary schools was renewed for another two years.

Whatever Johnson owed labour for its support in 1964 he strove to repay when in May of the following year he recommended Congress to amend Taft-Hartley so as to uphold the union-shop form of union security universally, by eliminating the provisions of its Section 14(b) which (it will be recalled) allow a weaker form of security if any state so decides. Enactment of that section in 1947 had been followed by a rash of so-called 'right-to-work' campaigns in many states. By 1965 nineteen of them had 'little Taft-Hartleys' permitting lesser forms of union security, down to virtually open-shop provisions which did not require a worker to join a union in order to keep his job. Repeal of 14(b), and of other anti-labour sections of the statute, had been advocated by the Democratic platforms of 1960 and 1964. According to a COPE spokesman, every candidate for national office in the latter year had been 'checked out on the matter of 14(b)' before endorsement. After Johnson's overwhelming victory, the labour lobby made repeal of this provision its top priority.

By means of intensive pressure and a deal with Congressmen from farm constituencies, repeal passed the House only to be defeated by a Senate filibuster in October. When the Administration tried again in 1966, attempts even to begin debate in that chamber were talked out. Meany angrily charged the Democrats with failure to deliver; but in fact the second bill's chances had not been improved by a fortnight's total strike of New York transport workers. The Supreme Court had felt bound meanwhile to uphold state courts in sustaining state laws where these limit or ban agency-shop agreements in labour-union contracts, and generally to deny the NLRB discretion to construe 'right-to-work' laws in senses more favourable to unions. Continuous turmoil over federal-state jurisdiction therefore still prevails in this field. It is not diminished by the circumstance that only a dozen states have their own labour relations boards and few possess machinery suitable in any way to resolve the matters with which Taft-Hartley deals. Wholesale evasion of the Act's ban on the closed shop in such industries as construction, printing and trucking, only partially mitigates the situation for labour.

Although AFL-CIO conventions repeat their biennial demand that Taft-Hartley be 'totally and drastically revised', the truth is that since 1954 no serious attempts have been made at a general overhaul. Indeed, if we except some safeguards provided by Landrum-Griffin for union security in the construction and garment industries, no bid for even partial amendment has of recent years succeeded. The federal courts have upheld its secondary boycott provisions on the whole restrictively: on the other hand their constructions have made a virtually dead letter of its limitations on feather-bedding. Where the Court has interpreted the statute to the greater freedom of unions, it is very doubtful whether this has contributed to industrial stability. For example, Section 301 of the Act permits either party to a labour-management agreement to sue in a federal court over contractual violation. Yet in June 1962 the Supreme Court held (in *Sinclair v. Atkinson*) that federal judges have no power to enjoin strikes called in breach of collective bargaining agreements; thus giving the Norris-La Guardia Act priority over Section 301 of the more recent Act despite the fact that nine-tenths of all contracts in 1962 contained clauses prohibiting strikes and requiring all disputes arising out of the contract to be settled through arbitration.

Indeed, the only part of Taft-Hartley for whose amendment the prospects are at the moment at all promising is that regarding strikes which constitute a national emergency. Here it is note-worthy that President Nixon (who himself helped to frame the original statute) has found the provisions for the President to obtain an eighty-day injunction and a temporary return to work quite inadequate. When invoked in 1959 in a vain attempt to cope with a steel strike which continued for 116 days, the emergency procedure was being resorted to for the sixteenth time in eleven years. In nearly fifty cases strikes have simply been resumed at the end of the 'cooling-off' period; and five times in the last ten years has Congress been obliged to inter-vene in such crises by imposing a compulsory settlement or otherwise. It is, therefore, possible that it will now give Nixon what his predecessors before him have requested – a more flexible variety of procedures for meeting such situations; perhaps some equivalent of the Presidential Emergency Board which has proved effective in comparable disputes on the rail-roads, who remain outside the scope of the 1947 Act. This prob-lem apart, however, it is clear that major changes in Taft-Hartley favourable to unionism must await massive shifts of political alignment; and of these there is no sign, but rather a lessening in the sense of urgency. The Act has at no time come anywhere near 'destroying' unions, though it has palpably slowed down or halted their organizing drives in areas where labour is weak, such as 'Operation Dixie' of the early 1950s. More than twenty years' experience, nevertheless, has convinced most observers of the need for a thoroughgoing Congressional review of labour-management law.

Meanwhile one cannot fail to notice the marked shift of emphasis during recent years in the American government's concern for workers, away from the labour force as a whole and towards particular sections of it deemed underprivileged – to urban dwellers, for instance, and above all to Negroes. The latter's demands for equal opportunity, ever more militant as they continue to flock citywards, have very naturally been raised in the field of employment, as well as housing, schools and elsewhere. It was a threatened march on Washington, organized by the Negro Brotherhood of Sleeping Car Porters, which persuaded Roosevelt to set up the first Presidential Committee on Fair Employment Practices in 1941. In 1960 Negro trade unionists formed a Negro American Labour Council whose platform called for the removal of all colour bars to union membership and parity in skill and seniority ratings. At the same juncture the National Association for the Advancement of Coloured People was intensifying its efforts before the courts. Within the executive branch, the President's Committee on Equal Employment Opportunity has today a very active labour advisory council. Congress, by Title VII of its Civil Rights Act of 1964, has forbidden colour discrimination by employers or employment agencies when hiring, firing or promoting, and by unions when admitting to membership. To enforce this provision in practice the Act set up an Equal Employment Opportunity Commission, whose hand the Civil Rights Act of 1967 has since strengthened with power to issue 'cease-and-desist' orders to combat discriminatory practices with speed. On the same day that the President signed the 1964 Act, the NLRB by its *Hughes Tool Company* decision made clear that it would withhold or withdraw its certification from any union which failed fairly to reflect the interest of all those workers, including Negroes, whom it officially represented when negotiating the terms of an agreement with management. More than half the states, as well as some municipalities, now also have Fair Employment Practice laws of their own.

Such measures, whether at state or federal level, have not of course changed the basic attitude – an antagonism on economic rather than racial grounds – of many white workers towards their 2m. black fellow-members, or persuaded many unions to add anti-discriminatory clauses to their constitutions. But they do provide legal and moral backing for the enlightened union leader seeking to carry egalitarian proposals not heretofore thought feasible. Nationally the AFL-CIO leadership has made exemplary efforts to eliminate disparity arising from colour, and by 1963 every affiliated union had abolished every formal trace of this on paper. On the other hand, labour's codes of ethical practice do not yet relate to the colour problem, and few individual unions have done much positively to improve the Negro's job situation where this objective has not been instrumental to their organizing or wage-levelling purposes. The unemployment rate for the black 11% of the American nation, though steadily falling, is still conspicuously above the national average, and rapid technological change, despite preferential training programmes, holds the Negro at a continuing disadvantage *vis-à-vis* the skilled white. With the recent removal of hurdles, such as the poll tax and unfairly administered literacy tests, from the Negro's path to the polling booth, labour's political programme more than ever needs his support. Yet, not surprisingly, many grounds for friction still remain between groups like the NAACP and labour organizations, which only 'good faith' practices by the latter can abolish.

Nor is it surprising that the Negroes have remained the most faithful component of the old Democratic coalition at a time when the election returns have been revealing some diminution, by abstention or leakage, of the labour vote as a whole. In November 1968, for instance, the New York city poll was down by some 480,000 from its 1964 figure; the Chicago poll by 240,000; and the Detroit by 137,000. Yet in particular city districts with large Negro populations the Humphrey vote held consistently around 80% of the total ballots cast. The attraction of George Wallace for some white blue-collar workers – an estimated 10% of them in the bigger cities – has been read as the index of resurgence of a populism as distinctly right-wing in 1968 as it had been left-wing twenty years before.

Whether this rightward swing will prove more than temporary it is too early to prophesy. Indeed, if this review of American labour's political concern through the last twenty years has seemed altogether too bare a record of electoral inputs and legislative outputs, the excuse must be that recent events lie too close for the eye to detect more sophisticated patterns. Nevertheless, some general trends and conditions can be distinguished. One may, for instance, safely suggest reasons why the last twenty years have for the USA constituted a period of remarkably steady economic advance. There has been the stabilizing effect of a consistently high level of government spending. Since 1950 the American economy has been in varying degrees on a defence footing. At the same time agricultural prices have been supported while domestic consumer demand has been sustained by the guaranteed benefits of social security.

Secondly, the general climate of the United States since World War II has clearly been one of conservatism. By 1950 the special Rooseveltian tone in politics was practically inaudible, and the nation became involved in what many Americans still conceive to be a continuous crusade against the forces of monolithic Communism. In industrial affairs, the short-lived public sympathy of the New Deal years towards labour has been displaced by something like the traditional suspicion, only now clothed in new forms. So far as popular feeling can be inspissated in precise statement, it would seem to be expressible as follows. What was once seen as labour's struggle against overmighty capital is nowadays a conflict between Big Labour and Big Business which carries its own threat to the ordinary public. Collective bargaining is viewed no longer as a method by which the workers seek (as in Gompers's time) to control their own job conditions, but as the way the two giants determine the conditions for joint control of a business, industry or service, in semi-isolation from those competitive forces by which the consuming public believe their interests to be protected. Many an American appears to feel, however inarticulately, that modern unions are inimical to the myth of consumer sovereignty. If they have curbed the autocratic power of the boss, it has been only through making him less responsive to the public by insulating him from the competitive pressures of the market. The citizen and voter has, therefore, been very ready to believe that the only way unions can be prevented from restricting competition in the interests of their own members and at the public expense is by governmental intervention. Hence the general support for controlling legislation.

Thirdly, though unions have not been able to stave off such legislation, neither have they been crippled by it. If liberals have not been numerous enough to prevent its passage, neither have conservatives been able to press it to the point of emasculating labour. The forces being fairly evenly matched, we must expect the recent period of deadlock or stalemate to continue. Meanwhile, much of the old animus has gone out of economic conflict. Deep emotional antagonism of worker towards employer has dwindled into a routine tension. Collective bargaining deals are likely to include employer-financed benefits such as supplementary contributions to union pension, welfare or health centre funds. For the young unionist today, union dues and political contributions are like premiums on an insurance policy designed to secure him protection against arbitrariness on management's part. His interest and involvement in union affairs are not great. Rising standards of education and wider diffusion of political information have induced in him a more independent attitude of mind towards public policies; while migration to the suburbs has relaxed the pressures of contiguity with his fellow unionists outside working hours.

This condition of relative tranquillity in union-management relations coincides with a period when organized labour in America is numerically at a standstill or in relative decline. Total union membership in the USA in 1968 was 18,843,000 – not a very significant increase over the 18·5m. of ten years earlier. This figure, particularly dampening to the hopes of the AFL-CIO from its remerger, shows moreover that unionism is not keeping pace with the growth of the American workforce. Losses have been heaviest in those declining industries traditionally the most densely unionized. In the last twenty years coal-mining and the railways have between them lost 1¼m. workers, while in the same period employment in the much less unionized service industries increased 90%. Unionization has fallen most significantly behind in the expanding white collar section, federal employees alone excepted. The prediction is that professional workers, of whom fewer than 10% are organized at present, will probably be the point of fastest growth in the immediate future, with the service industries – little more than 20% unionized – ranking second. The United States, it seems, is becoming less and less a labourer's country: but its trade unions are failing to keep pace with the continuing shift in the economy from goods to services. Can the AFL-CIO adapt itself to white-collar organization better than the AFL could to industrialized workers in the 1930s? Or will the USA ultimately be faced with two federations of labour, one for manual and one for non-manual workers, as in Sweden?

Parallel with this question runs that raised by the cumulative effect of technological progress. The lifting of recent recessions without perceptible lowering of the unemployment figures illustrates the speed at which the new automative revolution is proceeding. For the greater part of the 1960s, even though profits and production ran in most industries at record or near-record levels, the unemployment rate remained constant at about 5%. Merely to absorb new entrants into the American labour market would require an expansion of 25,000 jobs a week: but technology is rendering superfluous several hundred thousand more workers each year. Here the unions hardest hit are the big industrial ones, politically the most active and electorally the most strategically distributed. If they continue to dwindle, so will labour as a basis of support for the Democratic party.

To cope with these problems, forward looking and articulate labour leaders like the late Walter Reuther have long been pressing, in their testimony before Congressional committees and elsewhere, for greater formal co-operation between labour, industry and government, whereby the last of this trinity would commit itself to a programme of expansionary spending and a 'guaranteed income' policy for every citizen. Unhappily, differences of opinion about the urgency of such objectives have become one cause among others of the latest division in labour's ranks. Add to them the feeling that industrial unions have received less than their due meed of consideration within the AFL-CIO, particularly over their proper degree of representation on the federation's ageing executive council, together with the strong personal antipathy existing between Reuther and the seventy-five-year-old Meany, and the recent split becomes intelligible. After Reuther's Auto Workers had shown their dissatisfaction by withholding the union's dues from the parent body until well past the permissible date, the AFL-CIO was obliged in May 1968 to suspend the delinquent international from membership. Meany had indeed agreed to call a special national convention where the UAW's grievances and criticisms could be discussed; but Reuther would not agree in advance to be bound by its decisions. In the upshot, on 24 July following it was announced that the Auto Workers (1·8m. strong) would join with the 2m. Teamsters to form the Alliance for Labour Action (ALA). The AFL-CIO suffered a further defection in the following month when the 110,000 members of the Chemical Workers Union seceded to join the new body. What success can possibly attend a marriage of the highly centralized, progressive-minded Auto Workers with the decentralized, free-dealing Teamsters is to say the least unclear. A 10-cent per capita levy from all its members will give the ALA an estimated $4·7m. for its 'social action' fund, much of which will presumably be channelled towards political goals. But it is reasonable to fear, in the light of history, that labour's influence with the national government may – paradoxically, in view of Reuther's professed aims – be weakened by this new fission.

Thus internally divided, its membership threatened by large-scale technological obsolescence and lacking any corporate sense of mission, American labour faces the last three decades of the twentieth century with justifiable anxiety. Of one thing, however, it may be sure: while what it can secure at the bargaining table dwindles in significance with each passing year, the need for continuous political engagement bulks proportionately ever larger. Government is in the industrial field to stay, if only because of the general misgiving about trade unions as anti-competitive institutions within a theoretically competitive environment.

The kind of political engagement required, moreover, is of the pattern set by Hillman – not defensively self-seeking, but welcoming alliances with other liberal groups on behalf of all workers, and continuing to press for measures beneficial to every citizen. 'The union member,' proclaims the AFL-CIO's constitution, 'is first and foremost a citizen of his community.' 'The labour movement,' warned Reuther, 'can only be effective if it becomes less an economic movement and more a social movement.' More is needed of what Reuther, when head of the AFL-CIO's Industrial Department, was striving to do to improve the lot of the 'working poor' in marginal industries that have long suffered from union neglect. Only sustained political pressure on a broad front will foster that 'consumer-mindedness' among unionists which alone can break down barriers of suspicion between them and the general public and allow labour to pose convincingly as a genuine 'people's lobby'.

Whether, politically as well as economically, American unionism has already passed its apogee of power, only time will show. At the present juncture it may be more useful simply to note and evaluate the forms which its engagement in politics has so far taken.

6

Modes of engagement

'There are,' observed a Congressional committee on lobbying activities at mid-century, 'no significant interests in our society – economic, social or ideological – which do not in one way or another seek something from government.' Demands are the motive force of politics, and a myriad of what De Tocqueville called 'public associations' are engaged in making them. The US Department of Commerce's current handbook *National Associations of the United States* lists over 4,000 trade, professional and civic organizations, 'almost all' of which 'engage in lobbying to varying degrees'. In a highly differentiated modern industrial society, whose government is as fragmented as the American, this is natural. The First Amendment right 'to petition the government for a redress of grievances' makes it constitutional. The separation of powers, between a President who cannot certainly impose his will on Congress and a legislature which cannot hew policy to a coherent party line, makes it practically essential. 'Lobbying,' said the Congressional committee already quoted, 'is as habitual to our kind of government as breathing is to the human organism.'

'And,' they added, 'it is almost equally complex.' Surprisingly, no single comprehensive study exists of labour as a political pressure group. Its complexities, nevertheless, do admit of being approached in a systematic way. One may begin by noting the close *rapport* it has established over the last forty years with the executive branch. Even a Republican President will normally clear all his top labour appointments with leaders of trade unionism, and will ensure that it is represented on relevant Presidential committees and commissions. The Secretaryship of Labour may not always go to a trade unionist: but his Departmental staff will naturally be union-oriented, and unionists will collaborate in much of its advisory committee and council work. The AFL-CIO's civil rights department (to take only one example) nowadays works in close touch with the US Civil Rights Commission, the Community Relations Services of the Department of Justice, and the Civil Rights Compliance section of the Department of Health, Education and Welfare. Benefits are mutual. In the last year of the Truman administration more than seventy AFL and CIO members were on leave of absence from their unions in order to serve in agencies of domestic government, and a further sixty were officially representing the USA overseas. Reciprocally, the CIO's 1948 voting drive was launched when two hundred of its top brass were blessed by Mr Truman on the White House lawns.

But labour cannot expect the executive to be uniformly helpful at all junctures. The Department of Labour is always at the mercy of Congressional appropriations. It has never 'represented' the interest of workers in the same degree as the Department of Agriculture has that of farmers, or Commerce that of businessmen. A disgruntled union official at the time of the passage of Taft-Hartley went too far in asserting that Secretaries of Labour 'have never been real labour spokesmen, only glorified office boys in charge of labour statistics, speeches and other minor services'. Nevertheless, their Department probably commands the weakest 'constituency' strength of all Departments save only State, and has appeared as the main exception to the notorious tendency of American administration towards regulation of the regulators by the regulated.

Labour pressure, therefore, like that of most engaging groups, is focused chiefly upon Congress. There the labour groups with longest experience are of railroad workers; for the railways first and most clearly met the 'interstate commerce' conditions for governmental regulation. We have already noted Gompers's early National Legislative Committee, expanded in the 1930s into a National Joint Legislative Conference of AFL and

Railroads, and deriving continuity from the circumstance that one man, William C. Hushing, was its chairman from 1928 until 1955. Hushing's chairmanship also availed to link with this Conference the National Legislative Council which the AFL set up in 1949 after Taft-Hartley – a very large body upon which as many as a hundred representatives of every constituent section of the Federation might in emergencies claim a place, but with a normal working committee of nine.

At first the CIO relied for Washington representation upon the lobbyists of its individual affiliated unions. In 1942, however, it established a Legislative Department of a dozen specialists under a full-time director. The same officer was director also of the CIO Legislative Committee, a body composed of CIO vice-presidents and a dozen other top officials who, under Walter Reuther's chairmanship, exercised general direction of legislative policy. But the brunt of contact with legislators was borne by a small Legislative Operating Committee of twenty, comprising mainly the legislative agents of the fourteen component internationals, and meeting at least once a week during the Congressional session. Broadly speaking, if the Legislative Committee was concerned with general policy and the Legislative Department with strategy, then the Operating Committee's interests were tactical. Many of the CIO's early lobbying agents had served either in the administrative or legislative branches of the federal government; while one of the AFL's chief lobbyists in the early 1930s later became Assistant Secretary of Labour to Frances Perkins.

Re-merger of AFL and CIO in 1955 involved the welding of their lobbying activities into a single Department of Legislation, including five legislative representatives and directed since 1956 by a former Democratic Congressman from Wisconsin, Mr Andrew J. Biemiller. Policy continues to be formally resolved at the biennial conventions, in between which it is determined by the AFL-CIO executive council which also serves as the Committee on Legislation. An administrative committee, where the national legislative representatives are joined by another fifteen from affiliated unions and AFL-CIO departments, meets weekly to discuss legislative strategy and action in Congress, serving as a forum where information can be exchanged and activities co-ordinated. Once a month legislative representatives appointed by the presidents of affiliated unions and of the departments meet as the AFL-CIO Legislative Council, to discuss reports and other material prepared by the Department of Legislation on the status of pending bills. From time to time this council will be addressed by Congressional leaders and Administration officials.

Viewing this machinery in action we may distinguish three concentric circles. The innermost is formed by the small number of permanent, full-time agents in continuous contact with the Capitol, to whom it falls to prepare, in conjunction with any other relevant AFL-CIO department, a reasonable presentation of labour's views and to apply it at every necessary stage of the legislative process. In 1966, for instance, the Department of Legislation claimed to be concerned with more than 70 separate legislative issues, and in that year and the following to have made more than 110 formal appearances before Congressional committees; not to mention an incalculable number of informal contacts with individual legislators. Where a bill is not rated so highly, the Department may content itself with filing a written statement. Where on the contrary it is esteemed of first importance, the AFL-CIO president or secretary-treasurer may appear in person. In the Department's office are files on all relevant bills, together with voluminous notes on the attitude of every legislator – his reactions when approached, his voting, his public utterances inside Congress and out. These dossiers form an important section of the complete library of bills and resolutions, committee reports, calendars, transcripts of hearings, etc., which can be drawn upon when information is to be disseminated anywhere within the AFL-CIO. The Department also prepares and distributes a variety of materials including summary evaluations at the end of each Congressional session, fact sheets, and a 'Legislative Action Bulletin'.

This regular priming may prove invaluable when the second ring of legislative defence or attack – what the CIO used to call the 'Washington mobilization' – is resorted to. At a critical stage in the fortunes of a highly esteemed bit of legislation the Department may call on agents from all AFL-CIO internationals to converge upon the nation's lawmakers for several days of intensive interviewing.

The third and outermost ring is the Federation's ordinary

membership itself, whose pressure on any or all of their respective Congressmen or Senators may be invoked by the Legislative Department's issuing an 'action bulletin'. Great care must be exercised in this manoeuvre; and labour's lobby will normally prefer to encourage the local 'unofficial hearing', that is to say, the visit of like-minded constituents to legislators in their home states. All three rings of pressure were applied successively during the parliamentary career of the Taft-Hartley bill in 1947: but city-wide 'veto rallies' and repeal demands could not recover for labour the ground lost on Capitol Hill itself.

There exists, then, a field organization to buttress the claims labour makes upon legislators. Yet it does not follow that its effectiveness is proportional to the numbers engaged. The 'Coxey's march' on Washington, or 'petition in boots', as staged by the CIO in October 1945, is a foregone failure. Mass delegations are neither adept in the art of persuasion nor, on arrival, in the frame of mind to apply it. A Congressman, however susceptible to reasoned pressure in private, does not care to be publicly black-jacked into submission. Almost equally archaic is the 'push-button' mass letter or telegram lobby, with its artificial flood of stereotyped communications. Legislators are likely to be repelled by the mimeographed circular, the message on a form clipped from a labour newspaper, the bale of telegrams identical down to a common failure to spell 'amendment' correctly. A good illustration of such maladroitness occurred when Mr Carter Manasco, as chairman of the House committee considering the Murray employment bill of 1946, was the target:

Hundreds of duplicate CIO-PAC postcards reached Mr. Manasco's office one day telling him that if he did not use his influence to report out a strong Full Employment bill the signatories would vote against him in the next election. Manasco, who comes from the 7th District in Alabama, noted with interest that the cards were postmarked Brooklyn, New York.

The AFL-CIO's legislative department is nowadays more sophisticated, meticulously insistent that all grassroots pressure shall appear personal, the opposite of stereotyped:

Letters get more attention if they are not mass-produced. If you write your letter at a union meeting, see that a variety of stationery is used. Don't mail them all at one mailbox. Take your letter home and mail it at your local mailbox or post office.

Persons who organize meetings at which film strips are to be shown with the idea of stimulating letters should ask all workers attending to bring their own paper, envelopes and writing materials. In addition, for those who come unprepared, organizers should have on hand a supply of pencils with different kinds of lead and cheap ballpoint pens with different coloured inks. As wide a variety of writing paper and envelopes as possible should be kept available.

Different paper and envelopes and different qualities and colours of pencils and ink, however, are far less important considerations than the contents of each letter. Each should be individually written in the words of each individual letter writer.

Even thus supplied with materials and encouragement, however, it is the least educated – so the Gallup polls regularly show – who is least likely to respond by writing his representative. The prospect of mass lobbying may occasionally whet the appetite of labour's membership. But there is no substitute for the unspectacular professional agents. Those representing trade unions are as a class a little different from the majority of their ilk – probably older and having longer tenures, certainly paid less (their salaries must not get out of line with those of union officials in the plant), and more accustomed to regular collaboration with other minority groups.

On one thing, however, they will agree: that the most patently desirable time to serve their clientele is not when a Congress is packing its bags to leave Washington, but before it arrives there. The circumstances in which a candidate could secure labour's endorsement in Gompers's time is too casual for today. 'Reward your friends' – but too little care was taken to identify them and back them up. 'Punish your enemies' – but this was merely latching the stable door after Congress had bolted. Neither bestowal nor receipt of labour's cachet was taken very seriously by either side, and so what influence unionism exerted on the Hill suffered from being too loosely linked with support in the constituencies. One novelty of Hillman's PAC was the care it used to evaluate a legislator's actual performance on a number of 'key issues', in relation to his campaign promises, and to circulate the record to all unionists through regular 'voting guides'. Such compilations are now a regular feature of what is called political education: COPE claimed to have published and distributed 7m. copies in 1966. As to endorsements, only those for President and Vice-President are made nationally: the principle is that others should be made at the union level corresponding as nearly as possible with the electoral area the candidate seeks to represent. COPE's model by-laws emphasize the significance at any level of conferring formal recognition in this way. Some big internationals, such as the Auto Workers, make endorsements through their own national and state conventions, and Mineworkers and Railroad Brotherhoods likewise follow their independent procedures.

How important is the fact of endorsement? The hostile critic can easily find reasons for belittling it. The test votes selected by COPE can hardly amount to as much as one per cent of all those cast in a session. And of these, few may be really clear-cut. The experienced legislator displays great ingenuity in shuttling in and out of innumerable procedural amendments whereby he can probably 'vote right' enough times and yet be fundamentally unsympathetic to unions. Committees in particular may study to avoid roll-call voting on straight issues, so as to withhold ammunition from record compilers. Only groups with considerable weight at the polls can afford to risk the ire of a legislator who complains of an unfair selectivity. Because the process can be applied only to incumbents, moreover, it may operate in a conservative sense to disfavour the newcoming challenger. Outside of Congress, the number of districts where a pro-union stance is the *sine qua non* of success, though growing, is not great. The number of labour bodies, on the other hand, in any moderately industrialized district is likely to be enough to enable almost any candidate to claim the support of one of them. The most one can say is that the candidate who has received no labour cachet at all is likely to have tough sledding not only with unionists but with an indefinable number of liberally-minded

electors. In that respect the endorsement is not negligible.
And with it, one should add, a candidate may be better
able to link himself into the network of community organizations. For labour leaders are encouraged to participate with
other notables in a variety of civic, fraternal and public-spirited
groups within their localities and regions.

To correct and stabilize the worker's political vision requires
all-year-round attention. 'We have,' say COPE, 'as our first
responsibility the education of our membership on the issues
which we conceive to be of prime concern.' For this political
education the main channel is naturally the printed word;
whether in the regular periodicals – the *American Federationist*,
the *AFL-CIO News*, *Labour* (from the Railroad Brotherhoods)
and the 600 or so other organs of respective internationals and
areas – or of purely political sheets such as *Notes from COPE*,
or the monthly *COPE Report*, or the UAW's *Ammunition*. From
circulation figures in the *American Labour Press Directory* it
would seem that items in the former category of publication
enter nearly half of the American nation's 50m. households;
though, since they are economically speaking a 'dumped
product', that statistic is no infallible index of consumer demand. In the 1968 election campaigns, national COPE reckoned
that it had distributed in all more than 55m. pieces (not including
voting records), and guessed that about as much again emanated
from individual unions, state organizations, AFL-CIO central
councils and locals (for whose newspaper editors it runs regular
courses of instruction).

Is this tremendous output worthwhile? Printed literature is
by far the most expensive form of communicating with one's
membership and the most obviously subject to diminishing
returns. One way of justifying it is to point out that, by its angle
of vision and its selection of coverage, the labour press gives its
readers a picture of the political world radically different from
that painted by the American press at large. This is doubtless
valuable as a corrective and as in some small degree mitigating
the political one-sidedness inseparable from the latter's commercial monopoly. In the 1956 elections – to take a by no means
untypical example – a survey by the press's trade magazine, the
Editor and Publisher, showed 88% of daily newspaper circulation supporting Eisenhower; where in some states, and in

thirteen great cities, not a single daily was supporting Stevenson, labour's endorsee. Union publication, together with small-circulation liberal periodicals, may therefore help redress a considerable imbalance.

In so doing, however, it must borrow the weapons of its opponents by itself employing the stereotypes, the ripsnorting prose style and the packaged thinking of a Fulton Lewis, Jr. Who, for instance, reading in some union periodical of an 'anti-monopoly crusade', would pause to reflect that unionism is itself a most powerful and persuasive monopolistic form? Who, for that matter, could be sure that the periodical was not a mere puff-sheet of the incumbent union hierarchy? Too much of labour's propaganda, what is more, offers simplistic and pat solutions for complex contemporary problems, rigidly adhering to outmoded New Deal ideology – the 'screaming liberal line', which makes difficult compromise with either practical circumstances or potential allies.

What does it offer minority groups? A good 50% of membership in some of the garment unions are women. Ever since the PAC in 1946 set up a Women's Division, emulated by some internationals and state bodies, particular attention is paid to female readership; not merely because workers' wives are to be cherished as election day baby-sitters, telephone minders, and hostesses at 'meet-the-candidate' coffee hours, but because of the marginal weight women are (rightly or wrongly) believed to carry in some electoral areas. In others, the labour press will cater specially for coloured or foreign-language-speaking minorities, for whom COPE maintains a minorities department headed by a Negro.

What for the general public? Through twelve recent years the AFL-CIO sponsored the nightly newscasts of Edward P. Morgan over the ABC radio network. Its weekly 'Labour News Conference' – a series of interviews with union leaders over the Mutual Broadcasting System – continues into its ninth year. To the Department of Public Relations, too, falls the task of producing and distributing special films and tapes, in addition to its primary responsibility for dealing with the commercial press in all its aspects.

Much of the AFL-CIO's most effective propaganda, however, is shaped in conjunction with other of its standing committees

– on housing, education, social security, veterans' affairs, safety and occupational health, and civil rights – whose work the COPE then popularizes for electoral ends. From the AFL-CIO's legal department flow analyses of court decisions and NLRB rulings, for COPE to circulate in less technical and more polemical form. Since 1908 (incidentally) to the present day hardly a Supreme Court term has gone by without one appearance at least before it of the General Counsel of the AFL and, since 1938, of the CIO. One such General Counsel, Mr Arthur J. Goldberg, has gone on to a career of national and international distinction. Not least, the AFL-CIO's economic advisory staff supplies both COPE and the Legislative Department with those facts, figures and analyses that are their core material. Each big international adapts the output of its own research section to comparable uses.

What for its own militants? A very tiny fraction of labour's total gross literary output consists of specialized aids for its political organizers – speakers' handbooks, manuals of 'practical political action', guides to registration laws, 'debaters' kits', etc. This fodder for the bell-wethers of the flock is supplemented by instruction in conferences, schools or institutes, through which (it is claimed) thousands of the more politically conscious union officials pass annually, and some of which are held in Washington itself during the legislative season. In 1965 COPE began a series of 'Leadership Clinics', where officers of state and local COPE's were introduced to the techniques of electronic data-processing for use in their political programmes. While often the in-plant opinion leader most relied on is the shop steward, for 'on the knocker' evangelism in the electoral precinct itself labour has to recruit its missionaries where it can. In 1947 the PAC rhetorically announced its intention to raise 'a million blockworkers', and the following year LLPE set itself to plant 'a political trade union steward in every precinct of the United States'. Both targets were chimerical; but registration drives, spurred on by COPE's twelve area directors and two field representatives, are often pursued with real vigour and no little sloganizing:– 'Register to Vote: the Job You Save may be Your Own', 'Love Thy Neighbour – and Register Him', 'Bad Laws are made by Good People Who Don't Vote', 'A Worker Without a Vote is a Worker Without his Pants', etc.

The visitor to any big city COPE headquarters in September or October of an even-numbered year is likely to find much the same signs of activity. Several score girls will be handling Remington Rand or similar machines, filing the names, addresses, telephone numbers and union affiliation of most AFL-CIO members in that city and its suburbs. Cards, tapes or 'print-outs' are sorted topographically and then taken to the appropriate public registry office and checked against the Board of Elections' lists to ascertain each member's ward and precinct. Cards of members still unregistered will then be sent to the officers of their respective locals, perhaps to be further broken down by shop. A union member who remains still unregistered after a certain time may receive a reminder from a conscientious local officer or shop steward. COPE headquarters will also see that local officers and COPEs in its area are informed of laws governing registration there, and may also negotiate with Boards of Elections to secure the most favourable registration conditions possible. Sometimes a Board may be prepared to set up registration booths at factory gates. Sometimes union officers have been permitted to enrol as deputy registrars. Local COPEs may provide practical instruction for unionists in the use of the voting machine; may arrange with the city or county clerk for absentee balloting of sick workers; and for polling day itself may have recruited an army of poll-watchers, a fleet of chauffeurs to the polling station, a baby-sitting corps and a telephone brigade (including those professional bell-ringers, the Communication Workers of America). In 1968 COPE claimed credit for 4·6m. potential voters registered. In the week preceding the elections it reckoned to have mobilized over 191,000 paid workers throughout the nation, and on polling day itself nearly 25,000 recruits manning telephones and over 72,000 house-to-house canvassers getting out the vote.

From all this welter of political activity two conclusions emerge. The first, and most obvious, is that political engagement by organized labour in America today is no longer an anguished, spontaneous popular outburst, but a sustained effort, as nearly continuous as possible, to bring out an informed vote. The second, and less obvious, is that this effort is based on a handful of basic assumptions or postulates accepted as self-evident. We may examine some of these, and ask if they are really so.

10

The first postulate is what we may call the principle of poli-
tico-economic equivalence; that is to say, an assumption that
the institutions and means of economic action are by and large
those most appropriate to political action also. At every level,
as we have seen, from the AFL-CIO executive council down to
the shop steward, control of political activity tends to be vested
in the same hands that guide economic policy. This assimilation
of means is repeatedly and openly emphasized:

> It is to his union that the worker naturally looks for
> protection of his wages, hours and working conditions. It
> follows as day follows night that political, governmental
> measures having an impact on those same wages, hours and
> working conditions must also be approached by the worker
> *through his union*.
> A union is able to consummate a new agreement with the
> employer on satisfactory terms if it is strong. So similarly
> with LLPE.
> Political platforms are like union contracts. They only mean
> as much as we make them mean in the shop. Writing a letter
> to your Congressman can be as important to your personal
> welfare as filing a grievance with your shop steward . . . Any
> legislative request or protest you want to make must be
> handled *the same way* grievances or requests for union
> representation in other matters are handled in the plant.
> Basically there is little difference between organizing men for
> political action and organizing them into unions. The
> techniques are *the same*.

So are the idiom and vocabulary even:

> If we are to present a united front to our enemies there must
> be no political scabbery. An unregistered member anywhere
> is a political scab.
> The trade unionist who votes for a candidate who is not a
> dependable friend of labour is strike-breaking at the ballot
> box. Politically speaking, he is crossing the picket line.

Likewise the non-voting worker who reaps the benefit of the
electoral victory of a labour-supported candidate is a 'political
free-rider'; while for a worker to cast his ballot for a NAM-
supported one is 'political company-unionism'.

But is the assumption justified that institutions originally created for economic purposes can aptly subserve political ends also? For one objection, there is no necessary coincidence between the 'natural' areas of economic and political organization. Union bodies must accept electoral ward, precinct and Congressional district as they find them. Even the superficial correspondence between states as political entities and as levels of AFL-CIO structure does not go far. For not these latter, but the various internationals, jealous of any threatened usurpation of their authorities, have compulsory powers over locals in their areas; while city centrals and other groupings of labour bodies are under the surveillance of the national executive council of the parent federation.

Compartmentalization of political control suggests another contradistinction from economic. A union's economic strength grows in proportion to the strength of the whole movement, the organizing of each area making the adjoining area more vulnerable to union pressures. In contrast, the election of a liberal mayor in one city does not make either more or less likely the choice of a liberal mayor by its neighbour, nor does the return of a progressively minded Senator from one state necessarily conduce to a similar success in an adjoining state. A strong and active COPE in one district can do little or nothing, save by its shining example, to secure election of a good representative in another district. As in space, so in time. American politics are fluid and dynamic. There is no hope of a static organization such as is durably built up, brick by brick, when an economic empire is created. Strong showing made in one district, highly sensitive as it will be to shifting local interests and loyalties, will not suffice to secure the victors against challenge by a vigorous movement from the opposite direction in the next campaigning season. It will be clear that, while an economic victory by unionism 'stays won', a political victory will be only transitory unless sustained by continuous effort.

Yet in eliciting political effort from members, the union officer can bring to bear no such pressure as he can when underlining economic grievances. The latter are continuously felt in the shop, but political indignation is not easily kept on the boil. The economic pay-off of a strike is relatively immediate and obvious: not so the long-term amelioration through politics. Loyalty to

10*

a union leader is an apprehensible thing: loyalty to a politicia is not. Most workers are not visionaries. The America they know is fundamentally right enough.

The second and third postulates of labour's political actio are neither of them conclusively provable or disprovable b argument or demonstration. But are they mutually compatible One is that, while preserving some local bargaining freedom labour's interests are best served by seeking a stable relationshi with the Democratic party. The other, that worthwhile politic is the politics of 'issues', not personalities.

The *rapport* which organized labour has since 1933 main tained with the Democrats is apparent at all levels of that party Its quadrennial national convention is likely to see 300 to 40 union representatives present as delegates or alternates, th Republican convention less than a dozen. The labour-supporte Republican candidate is exceptional. The Republican dynastie who used to head the old AFL construction unions are almos extinct; and since the New Deal the trade unions have been, an still largely are, a reliable component of an increasingly shak Democrat coalition. In consequence, labour's electoral effi ciency, measured solely by the percentage of victorious candi dates, has for the last thirty years closely paralleled the ebb an flow of that party's fortunes. This general circumstance, how ever, does not imply the existence of a single, normative rela tionship, save perhaps in Minnesota where the Democratic Farmer-Labour party is officially recognized as a regula protagonist. Mutual attitudes will vary with relative mutua strengths from area to area of the nation. Where unionism i exceptionally strong – Michigan with its high concentration o Automobile Workers is a rare example – it may not only suppl the bulk of election dollars and workers, but actually enter th Democratic party and either take it over or considerabl modify it from within. Where unionism is locally weak it ma confine itself to a satellite role. Where moderately strong an efficient, it will probably seek to influence the party from without, perhaps to the extent of a trial of strength in the early stages of an electoral contest – for instance, by building ar independent political organization and running a rival can didate of its own in the primaries – in the confidence that a good showing will have the desired impact on party policy.

But how far can labour's Democratic affinities be reconciled with what we have distinguished as a third postulate of its political action – that prime importance should be accorded 'issues' rather than men or labels? The CIO-PAC, for example, declared its aim to be

> progress towards the clear alignment of liberal and conservative forces and towards the further development of an electorate that will decide between candidates on the basis of issues and not on the basis of party labels.
> Labour can establish a new voting habit with American workers, namely the habit of voting for ideas. The particular party allegiance that will develop out of this habit is still unpredictable but the formation of this habit is basic.
> The net result is that the distinctions in political philosophy between the two major parties become more clear-cut . . .
> This, I think, is one major change taking place in the life of the nation which has been brought about by labour's political activity. I believe we can force the reactionaries of both old parties to form their own third party. Then labour can sit down and rebuild one of the two remaining parties supporting the liberals who stay on. Following such a political realignment the American people can vote for a clear-cut liberal programme with the full knowledge that when elected that party will carry out its liberal programme without qualification, compromise or delay.

There is of course nothing new about the American liberal's dream of clearly dichotomizing the two parties on respectively conservative and progressive bases. Only for a number of reasons it is, on a national scale, highly unlikely. Indeed, in all branches of government it seems harder nowadays to classify such-and-such a policy, action or ruling as distinctly 'liberal' or 'conservative' in the sense current in the Roosevelt era when labour first began regular and systematic political intervention. If such a polarization were ever achieved, moreover, it is likely that the Democrats, as the party of progress or change, could look forward to only few and brief periods of ascendancy.

One effect of this harping on issues may be, it is true, here and there to pull Democratic organizations a little more to the left. But another effect is certainly to create some mutual distrust and friction. Labour is prone to blame the defeat of a Democratic candidate on the shortcomings of 'party hacks'. Following the 1948 elections, officials of CIO-PAC and LLPE complained that

> most of the Democratic party state organizations throughout the country did not think they had a chance, and when they elected governors, and when they elected county tickets, it was the old story of putting their families back on the payroll. These fellows are no good to us. They will milk the thing for four years and not much will be done.
> We found the Democratic leadership in too many places too resentful of us or afraid of us. They do not want any part of us . . . The entrenched Democratic organization is afraid that the labour people are trying to take them over, and they are going to do everything they possibly can, of course, to prevent that.

Likewise its disappointments in the Congressional elections of 1950 labour afterwards laid at the door of

> the leaders of the Democratic party, who . . . gave us a lot of political hacks instead of men of great standing.
> It taught us that we should let no political organization just give us a candidate and tell us we can take it or leave it.

New York city union leaders complained of the 1960 campaigns:

> We are tired of being taken for granted, of being handed candidates we have to take without consultation, and of being ignored once the election is over.

Failure to turn the trick for Humphrey in 1968 labour blamed on dissident or apathetic party organizers:

> In a majority of states labour did the job alone, meeting the challenge with its own financial resources and manpower, for the Democratic party was either unable or unwilling to mount an effective effort to meet its political responsibility.

All this, however, and more in the same vein, cannot disguise the mutual need of unionists and Democrats for each other. The arguments against forming a third party of labour, which we noted at the outset (Chapter One), remain as valid today. In only one area of the country does a unique geographical concentration of industrial, ethnic and cultural affinities allow the needle trades unions to head a Liberal Party of New York; and that serves principally as a bargaining counter with the major parties there. Labour's left wing may grow restive, but they have nowhere to go. The officers of fifteen CIO unions in 1948 quietly diverted work and money towards Henry A. Wallace, but did not risk the wrath of their rank-and-file by endorsing him openly. In recent years the pull on the unionist has been towards the right, as support for the other Wallace in 1968 has shown. Yet propaganda and official pressure between them held most members firm for Humphrey. Despite periodic signs of strain, it does not look as though labour's traditional links with the Democratic party will break in the foreseeable future.

The flight of some blue-collar workers to George Wallace, however, does bring into question a fourth postulate underlying labour's political engagement, which is that its potentially greatest asset as a pressure group is its numerical voting-power. This carries the corollary that, if only its mass membership are well-informed and brought to the polls, they will always 'vote right'. The assumption about mere numbers is *prima facie* plausible. Totting up membership of the AFL-CIO, Auto-workers, Teamsters and Railroad Brotherhoods, and deducting those below voting age or outside the USA a reasonable estimate is 15 million. Adding their adult families, and retired members, the total vote which the unions might potentially sway could be as high as 25 million – nearly one-quarter of all Americans entitled to the franchise and more than one-third of the number who customarily exercise it.

Leaving on one side for the moment the unions' success or otherwise in getting their members to ballot at all, we may notice the ancillary assumption regularly proclaimed by their political organizers:

> If you can get them to the polls, our experience has shown that they will vote right 90%. There is no question in my mind about that.
> In case you don't know it already, the difference between a small vote and a big vote is the difference between a bad Congress and a good Congress. A big vote is always a good vote for democracy.

The bigger the vote the better the government.
We believe that on those occasions when the democratic
process failed to return a progressive verdict it was because
too few Americans participated in rendering that verdict.
Our slogan has always been that a big vote is a progressive
vote. We still stick by that slogan.
When Americans flock to the polls in large numbers they
elect progressive, independent candidates.
The bigger the vote, the more pro-labour candidates get
elected.
It can be stated virtually as dogma that the larger the vote the
better is the liberal candidate's chance of winning.
The only trouble with people in politics is that there aren't
enough of them.

Heavy polling is contrasted with the traditional state of affairs
where a local boss deliberately restricted voting numbers in the
interest of his own control of the machine. A small poll is the
symptom of the old-line machine at work: whereas 'the major
purpose of labour's political action is the achievement of a
maximum vote, and this concept is the antithesis of machine
politics'.

Reliance on its numerical strength, however, makes labour
the most conspicuous among contending political groups. Of all
such groups it must, therefore, be most on its guard against
flaunting the dubious weight of numbers, for excessive militance may not only split its own membership but create anti-
labour backlash. Its political organizers cannot risk forfeiting
the goodwill of uncommitted liberals by words or deeds that
may give the impression of a 'labour bloc'. Their tactics, on the
contrary, must be tailored with care to suit the constituency. A
handbill proclaiming 'Labour's United League' in large letters
may go down very well in a working area but is too blatant for a
'silk-stocking' ward. The over-strident tone of PAC activities
in Ohio in 1950 played into the hands of Taft, who could the
more plausibly denounce CIO 'invaders' and 'carpet-baggers'.
'The power of labour' is a heady concept: very few Americans
are neutral to it. The standing in Washington of Senator Pat
McNamara was probably not enhanced by his being introduced
at union conventions as 'labour's own Senator'. Towards power

in politics the labour leader's attitude must be ambivalent. To party politicians he must convey the maximum impression of vote-carrying weight. Yet to the public his organization must be represented as David facing the Goliath of the great corporations.

Confidence in numbers, whether well-founded or not, has some bearing upon a fifth postulate of political engagement, which is that, while some classes of legislation are admittedly more important to workers than others, labour, fortified by the size of its potential voting power, does best to engage on a broad front. In its width of political programme, commensurate almost with the whole gamut of economic and social issues, it is unique among pressure groups. In view of the notorious weakness of consumers' pressure groups, this breadth would seem to be advantageously filling a gap.

In practice, however, labour's extended front is vulnerable at too many points to highly concentrated counter-pressures from agencies which do not dissipate their energies by attempting to 'shoot for the whole works', but focus them selectively on clearly defined goals. Arrayed against unionism on the economic sector are the National Association of Manufacturers and the U.S. Chamber of Commerce – to mention only the two largest of their kind. At the peak of their success over Taft-Hartley, the former claimed to enfold 16,500 corporate members, the latter about 21,500 business firms. Between them today they also co-ordinate the efforts of over five hundred lesser national trade associations.

Over issues of social policy labour's position is countered, point by point, in greater detail. In the sphere of health, for instance, the labour lobby's support of a comprehensive federal insurance scheme was long and relentlessly opposed by the American Medical Association, whose compulsory levy upon its membership sufficed to keep it atop the list of reported lobby spenders – to say nothing of its outlay in moulding public opinion – for three successive years during its struggle with the Truman administration's health plans. Similarly, labour's support of federal public housing programmes has met the concentrated resistance of (among other real estate groups) the National Association of Real Estate Boards. The activities of NAREB's highly developed lobby – the Realtor's Washington Committee of 600 to 700 'contacts' on behalf of NAREB's 54,000 members – were a prime reason for the establishment of a Congressional committee to investigate lobbies in 1950. In the domain of public power likewise, labour must contend with a formidable private power and utilities lobby, dominated by the National Association of Electric Companies. Labour's attempts under the Republicans to secure public ownership of oil and natural gas resources were overborne by private commercial lobbies: ironically it was the attempt by one of these to buy a Senator's support for a natural gas bill in 1956 that led directly to the setting up by the Senate of the McClellan special investigatory committee whose report led to further restrictions upon trade unions.

Some features of labour's political activity both business and the Republican party have sincerely flattered by imitation. The latter's national committee in 1954 announced plans for an 'action school' in Washington for party workers from all over the country, and for an 'action committee' to compete with CIO-PAC and LLPE. Then independent Republicans set up their Effective Citizens Organization, a non-profit group designed to stimulate greater participation by businessmen in electoral politics. In 1958 the National Association of Manufacturers created its own political action committee and the US Chamber of Commerce its Special Committee for Voluntary Unionism: both have run 'action courses in practical politics' for business executives. By the end of 1960 it was estimated that a quarter of a million businessmen had been exposed to instruction of this kind under the auspices of one firm or another. Numerous 'Citizen's Committees' are palpably supported by large industries; and the 1950s saw the appearance of many a pamphlet bearing a title such as 'Business in Politics – How Far You Can Go'.

If these enterprises have not greatly flourished, it is because this mode of engagement is not really appropriate to the businessman. Doorbell ringing and envelope stuffing are not his *forte*; nor does local politics, in which labour unions are rooted, concern him to the same degree. Business naturally exercises more effective pressure at other levels and by other means. One of these means is money, at whose importance in elections we must now look from labour's point of view.

Among groups who regularly report how much they annually lay out on lobbying Congress, the AFL-CIO is usually to be found in the top three or four spenders, at a present level which is fairly steadily around $160,000 a session. Amounts spent by other labour organizations or individual unions fluctuate widely, according to legislation pending. A special legislative campaign (for example) mounted in 1966 by one AFL-CIO international, the United Federation of Postal Clerks, made that union top lobby spender for three successive years. But this is exceptional: wide fluctuations from year to year are on the whole more typical of non-labour groups. In 1965 the American Medical Association's reported outlay in an attempt to defeat a Medicare bill leapt from its 1964 figure of below $46,000 to one of over $1·1m.

But all such figures are robbed of significance by the notorious inadequacy of the statute still governing federal lobbying. The La Follette-Monroney Act of 1947 requires reports of lobbying expenditures to be filed with officers in each house of Congress, but does not require the latter to act on the reports; so that prosecution under the Act is virtually unknown. Moreover, test cases before the US Supreme Court in the early 1950s so reduced the Act's scope that reporting is now obligatory only for those organizations which actually solicit or receive (not simply *spend*) money for the *principal* purpose of influencing legislation by *direct* and continuous communication with federal legislators. This narrow construction has enabled (for instance) the National Association of Manufacturers – no political eunuch – to escape without having filed a lobbying report since 1950. Furthermore, as a Congressional committee investigating lobbying observed in 1950, 'it is less than realistic to confine the principle of full disclosure to lobbying activities on the legislative level when an increasing proportion of these activities are taking place elsewhere'. A group can spend a million dollars in any year on 'public opinion moulding', by advertising and otherwise, without being obliged to report anything to anybody.

Reported figures of campaign expenditures possess slightly more significance but not much. Federal statutes limiting the amount any organization can give to national candidates or their campaign committees apply only to bodies operative in two or more states. Hence there is much decentralization whereby national headquarters of fund-raising associations pass on money to their state counterparts (operative under distinct names) and report only that proportion they themselves retain and spend. Before looking at the monetary resources available to organized labour for electoral campaigning, it is necessary to understand the restrictions laid by federal law upon their use for that precise purpose.

The United States has no party that rests, like the Labour Party of Britain or the Social-Democrats of West Germany, upon a stable basis of union dues-payers. But until less than thirty years ago a trade union's freedom to contribute money to national candidates or their committees was limited only by general legislation such as the Federal Corrupt Practices Act (of 1925, as amended in 1940), into the efficacy of which we do not go here, but which left any union free to contribute from its general funds up to $5,000 apiece to candidates for national office and to national campaign committees. The Smith-Connally Act of 1943, however, included a section specifically aimed at Lewis's Mineworkers, those large contributors to the Democrats in 1936 (see pp. 67 and 79 above). That section declared it henceforth illegal for any labour organization (as it already was for any business group) to make financial contributions from its ordinary fisc in connection with the election of US President, Vice-President, Senator or Congressman, and for any such candidate or national political committee to accept them. It was in strictest compliance with this law that Hillman's CIO-PAC, and indeed PACs at all levels, kept separate from its main account those moneys voluntarily contributed by unionists, through 'dollar drives', for directly aiding candidates and conducting electoral propaganda. Only the cost of all-year-round political education was met out of general funds. Notwithstanding, labour spent more money nationally in 1944 – an estimated $1,570,000 – than in any previous election; before Taft-Hartley, again ostensibly equalizing labour with business in the eyes of the law, in 1947 extended the discriminatory ban to include electoral 'expenditures' (a crucial word) as well as contributions, and to cover earlier stages of election too. Later incorporated in the Federal Corrupt Practices Act of 1958 as Section 610, the prohibition, which is backed by penalties of fine and/or imprisonment, reads (the italics showing what Taft-Hartley added):

It is unlawful . . . for any corporation whatever, *or any labour organization*, to make a contribution *or expenditure* in connection with any election at which Presidential or Vice Presidential electors or a Senator or Representative in . . . Congress are to be voted for, *or in connection with any primary election or political convention or caucus held to select candidates for any of the foregoing offices*, or for any candidate, political committee, or other person to accept or receive any contribution prohibited by this section.

As LLPE and COPE were successively formed, each had, therefore, to imitate the CIO-PAC in the compartmentalizing of its campaign chest so as to ensure that no strictly electoral expenditures in connection with national candidates are made out of any union's general funds. A standard procedure was evolved by COPE for the 1956 electoral year which has been followed ever since. Under this, each constituent union of the AFL-CIO is asked to raise from its locals a biennial quota equivalent to twenty-five cents per head of membership. Half of this quota money is later returned for use in the state of origin. At the same time, voluntary contributions are sought from unionists through dollar drives, the proceeds of which go into a segregated account. As COPE gets into state elections, the quota (or 'educational') account is drawn on; then, as national campaigns open, the voluntary contribution account. Federal elections over, the costs of 'political education' revert to the quota account; and then to the AFL-CIO's general funds, upon which are borne the year-round administrative costs and salaries of COPE. Altogether then, there exist today three sources of political money for the AFL-CIO, one of which – voluntary contributions – is legally unrestricted as to use. Which of the other two sources – quota account or general funds – is drawn upon at any time seems to be a matter of electoral exigency or practical convenience. Parallel distinctions are preserved in any arrangement by which certain AFL-CIO inter-nationals – railroad unions, mineworkers, garment workers, and a few others – raise and spend political money independently of the parent federation.

A few individual American states have laws imitating all or part of Section 610, but none of these has aroused the same amount of controversy as the federal model. Of this controversy the seeds were buried during the confused debating of Taft-Hartley in Congress. The buds have been opening in the federal courts ever since. One is the question whether a union's ordinary publications, printed and distributed out of its general funds, may legally include matter supporting or opposing particular national candidates at election times. In a case of 1948 (*US v. CIO*) the Supreme Court ruled that Congress had not meant its ban to apply to trade journals issued by unions or corporations 'in the regular course of conducting their affairs' to those 'accustomed to receive them', advising them 'of danger or advantage to their interests from the adoption of measures, or the election to office of men espousing such measures'. Unions in the 1948 national campaigns appear to have taken full advantage of this freedom to spend on political literature from non-voluntary funds. One Connecticut local in that year met out of non-voluntary funds the small cost of a local radio broadcast urging the defeat of Republican candidates, and got away with it in a circuit court of appeals (*US v. Painters' Local 481 (AFL)*) as a 'natural' way of communicating its views to its members where it owned no newspaper. A less favourable view, however, was taken by the Supreme Court (in *US v. United Automobile Workers (CIO)*) where during the mid-term campaigns of 1954 the Automobile Workers spent nearly $6,000 from its general funds on a television broadcast in support of Democratic candidates over a commercial station. A Pipefitters Union local in Missouri suffered a clear conviction under Section 610 in 1968. Clearly, both the size of a union's audience and of its expenditure have been factors influencing judicial views about the scope of the legal ban.

Another related point of controversy has been the degree of monetary protection to be afforded minorities within unions and the individual unionist himself (whom Taft-Hartley's framers were ostensibly concerned to protect) against majority decisions in political matters. Protesters have urged the right of the worker not to have any part of his compulsory payments (initiation fees, dues, levies) used to further a political cause with which he disagrees. With this view the Supreme Court (in

International Association of Machinists v. Street (1961) and *Brotherhood of Railroad Clerks v. Allen* (1962)) has concurred. But the general difficulty is hard to resolve categorically, since political engagement, as we repeatedly see, may nowadays be as vital to workers' welfare as economic action, majority decisions on which are legally held to imply the consent of all.

Most of the court cases mentioned above have touched if not turned on the 'First Amendment freedoms' of trade unions and their individual members. But they have often raised a more technical question as well. At what point exactly does 'political education' (definable as the inculcation of broad socio-political attitudes among sections of the electorate) involving the publication and circulation of factual matter such as a Congressman's voting record, shade off into propaganda on behalf of a particular candidate or candidates? It has been hard to say. But the courts have usually opined (as did Senator Taft when defending his bill in Congress) that Section 610 permits a union to use its general fund for the former kind of activity but not the latter. The rationale supporting this distinction seems to be that when unions under their own clearly avowed auspices express their views on political issues, as distinct from paying for a favoured politician to broadcast his own, their constitutional right of free speech is suitably tempered in the public interest. Canvassing for particular candidates, and polling-day work on their behalf, must be paid for solely out of the proceeds of voluntary contributions: canvassing of issues, and registration drives as a public service, need not.

Much of labour's routine 'educational' work in politics, then, is quite legitimately financed out of general funds. For this purpose the LLPE began in 1949 to raise a 10-cent per capita levy from AFL members. Nowadays the national AFL-CIO spends about $1m. annually on the administrative expenses of COPE – as much as it spends on all public relations – and in election years may allocate another $\frac{1}{4}$m. to COPE's voter registration fund, to which individual unions probably add another $\frac{1}{2}$m. The Auto Workers maintain a 'Citizens' Fund' for which 5% of their members' dues are earmarked at national and local levels. By similar means the expelled Teamsters support their 'Democrats, Republicans and Independents for Voter Education' (DRIVE) as a political stimulant.

This distinction between 'educational' and 'political' activity is a precarious and often sophisticated one. Even allowing for basic differences between British and American campaigning, there might seem something to be said for adoption in the United States of a device comparable to the distinct political fund of the British trade union, earmarked for *any political use whatsoever*, but with provision for the individual to contract either in or out. A mere seven years' experience of Section 610 sufficed to convince the US Department of Justice that it was 'almost impossible, certainly impractical, to prosecute under'. If it is a fiction, however, it is one which does not seem to handicap either business or labour. It has not reduced unions to desperation, and corporations have other ways of raising the wind.

Voluntary subscription remains of all modes of political engagement the least popular with unionists. For its first election campaigns COPE in 1956 asked each constituent AFL-CIO union to try to raise by this means a sum equivalent to one dollar a head of 25% of its membership. The sum in fact raised was reported as $1,118,000. Although the totals subscribed in subsequent campaign years have been nominally higher, they still represent less than a dime a head of membership. Clearly, then, this constitutes no great threat to business. One specialist in campaign finance, Professor Alexander Heard, calculates that the above-mentioned sum raised by COPE in 1956 from 16m. AFL-CIO members was comfortably surpassed by the total gifts of individual members of only twelve wealthy (and Republican) families. When, however, we add to it the direct campaign spending of all labour groups, the aggregate reported outlay looks more formidable – some $4·3m. (to take the 1966 figures) from forty-two groups. If this be added to the reported expenditures by or for national Democratic candidates in that year, it may have given the latter party the monetary edge over its rival. In the Presidential year of 1968, however, when labour's reported contributions to the campaigns of national politicians reached a record total of $7·6m., equivalent to over half the reported expenditures of all national Democratic fund-raising committees, Republican receipts and expenditures had forged well ahead again.

Exceptionally, some of the money contributed by labour for

political campaigning goes to other groups. For part of the 1950s, for instance, the Ladies Garment Workers were donating about $15,500 on annual average to Americans for Democratic Action. But most such payments are made to parties, and, since 1936, the Democrats have received the lion's share. On the same specialist's calculations, throughout the 1950s about one-seventh part of the direct expenses of pro-Democrat committees at national level was being met with labour money. But union leaders prefer on the whole to deal in financial matters immediately with candidates rather than with party committees; and a second expert has plausibly reckoned that as much as 25% of Democratic funds at all levels in a campaigning year may derive from unions. There is evidence that during the 1960s COPE and other such organs were learning to focus their cash outlays more selectively on a smaller number of constituencies where their impact would be most critical.

Viewing it as a whole, we need to keep the problem of labour's political spending in due scale and proportion. Voluntary contributions aggregate annually no more than three-tenths of one per cent of what American unions collect in dues, and even their levies for 'political education' realize appreciably less than five cents a member. Professor Heard concludes that although 'a great deal of union dues money is spent on activities that are intended to affect the outcome of federal and other elections, and presumably do', yet 'labour money in politics from all sources pays a much smaller share of the nation's campaign-connected costs than union members constitute of the population of voting age'. A still broader perspective convinces one that money is, and always will be, only a small component of the total influence which organized labour exerts on the outcome of American elections.

How can we begin to assess this total influence? Organized labour is certainly not a monolithic force in American politics. Many of its leaders try to stay out of partisan election campaigns, and many of its members vote contrary to the public endorsements of their unions. Studies of workers' voting habits show that even in Michigan as many as 20% of the Auto Workers may at times be opposed to their union's political stance. This recalcitrance may spring partly from the principled belief that a man's politics are his own private business, partly from a fear, surviving from Gompersian days, that open political commitment may impair the union's flexibility in economic bargaining. More often, however, disaffection from an official line stems from some divisive factor. This may be a simple partisan one, such as traditional allegiance to the Republican party. After sampling voters' intentions in 1950 in Ohio, where labour propaganda against the abhorred Senator Robert A. Taft had been intensive, the American Institute of Public Opinion reported that well over one-third of union members questioned there were willing to state their preference for the Republicans. Partisanship may be reinforced by personalities. Even in Detroit in 1952 a minority of 25% of workers interviewed confessed to having voted Eisenhower into the Presidency contrary to the official stand of the UAW. In that same year three presidents of AFL internationals openly canvassed the Republican ticket, and in 1956 five opposed the re-endorsement of Adlai Stevenson. A careful estimate of the proportions in which white blue-collar workers in larger cities split their vote in the 1968 Presidential contest suggests 47% for Humphrey, 43% for Nixon, and 10% for Wallace, who attracted particular support from the lower income white precincts of those cities.

For race may be another cause of fission. Southern employers have long been able to play on racial sentiment to keep unions down there from achieving full solidarity; and of late years COPE has lamented the refusal of many unionists all over the country to support 'open housing' planks of its civil rights programmes. Or religious:— Catholicism is a sharp divisor in the matter of federal aid to education. Nor must one forget the fissiparous political effects of localism in the United States, where parochial issues may easily supervene over national goals. A city of moderate size may contain locals of more than sixty different unions, providing a fertile field for rivalries, jurisdictional and otherwise. The old craft and construction unions are particularly tied to locality, being deeply concerned about municipal building programmes and codes. Printing unions want the city's printing done by local firms. All workers want forbearance by the police towards striking and picketing, and a sympathetic relief administration when funds run out.

Probably the greatest threat of all to labour's political unity, however, is nowadays a topographical one – the flight of workers to the suburbs and the modification of their political outlook by 'social absorption' there. This flight became accelerated after World War II by the availability of low-cost loans from the Federal Housing and Veterans Administrations. Depopulation and impoverishment of the city centres, where Negroes chiefly congregate, are by now familiar consequences. An investigation undertaken in 1966 (the Kraft survey) showed nearly 50% of all union members, and 75% of members under the age of forty, to be resident in suburbia, whose population has continued to grow disproportionately and whose electoral weight has been increased by redistricting.

This phenomenon confronts labour's political organizers with a double problem. As soon as the work-shift ends, a plant's labour force may scatter rapidly over an area of several hundred square miles. How can organizers muster a solid vote through precinct organizations designed to work within cities, not miles outside of them? Most of the suburban COPE organizations already in existence started as *ad hoc* groups formed to deal with such immediate and parochial problems as stop lights, freeways, zoning divisions and bond issues. Old political action techniques formerly employed in pursuit of state and national goals have now to be adapted to help a new kind of union member solve a new kind of problem. Secondly, the greater the physical separation of a worker's place of work from his place of residence, the greater the emotional separation also. In the new suburbs he, and even more his wife, is exposed to a pervasive social ambience inclining him to vote to the approbation of his neighbours rather than of his union officiate. Suburbs, as labour leaders recognize, are the new frontier of politics. Recognizing the elementary necessity to 'go where the members live', COPE has recently undertaken some pilot projects aimed at discovering how best to counter this novel threat to electoral solidarity. It is one which, at the very least, serves to illustrate and re-emphasize the variety of cross-pressures – social and ethnic, civic and local – to which every unionist is constantly subject.

Other aspects of union membership, beside this heterogeneity, must influence the way their political organizers approach them. One consideration is that of age. The 1966 survey revealed that 25% of all American unionists were less than thirty years old and nearly 50% were under forty. These figures, though un-surprising in themselves, serve to stress how few workers have any recollection of depression, New Deal or World War. The old emotive legends leave them unmoved. Another considera-tion is the wide spread of workers' incomes today. The 1966 survey showed that 32% of union families are in the $5,000–7,000 a year range and 46% in the $7,500–15,000. In fine, union organizers are nowadays trying to serve a constituency one-half of which is under the age of 40, living in the suburbs, and taking for granted unprecedentedly high incomes. These are likely to be less interested in what past political action has won in the way of union security, social insurance and so on, and more concerned with such matters as air pollution, better recrea-tional facilities, 'truth in packaging', cheaper automobile in-surance, etc. They are moving rapidly towards the politics of affluence. Well might COPE recently plug the electoral slogan: 'To live like a Republican, vote for a Democrat'.

On these and other of the worker's prejudices political leader-ship must be brought to bear selectively, attempting to reinforce them where favourable and modify them where not; and above all to develop the latent tendency into the concrete vote. Suc-cess in doing so will obviously depend on local variables, many of which are not within the political organizer's control. A local's membership, for instance, may be neither fully agreed nor fully articulate as to its real needs; or these may be overlaid by dominant pressure from outside the area, from the head-quarters of its international. Local union leaders may be without previous experience of political action, may be locked in fratricidal conflict, or lack good channels of communication with their rank-and-file, whose attendance at mass meetings is unlikely to be on average higher than that of their British confrères.

By now, however, a sufficient number of area case studies are available for students to judge how successfully or otherwise COPE and similar bodies impinge upon union membership. Their conclusions, which are fairly uniform and in their gener-ality rather platitudinous, can only be summarized here. They are that, where the job of political education is well done, unionists' perception of their leaders' attitudes is sharper and, therefore, more influential. Where political objectives have been clearly formulated, the criteria relevant to the choice to be made at the polls are better understood. Clearer perception of issues leads to greater appreciation by workers of their economic and social stake in politics, and this in turn to higher political interest, greater exposure and deeper involvement. To say the least, political involvement has been found to be much stronger among unionists than among comparable non-union people. It is also concluded that, his interest once aroused, the union member, however high his wage, is more likely than the non-unionist to identify himself with a viewpoint that, for want of a better designation, must be called working class.

What does all this amount to in the practical outcome? Nothing that we had not already been led to expect. Indifference or opposition to political engagement is still considerable and may in unfavourable circumstances rise to a peak of between 40% and 50% of a local's membership. This curve is closely paralleled by those representing the proportion of unionists who claim not to have been reached by their union's political propaganda and the proportion who report themselves as not playing much part in union affairs as a whole. Conversely, the more strongly union-oriented the worker, the likelier he is to vote. And political involvement is most visible when it takes the form of voting for a Democratic candidate. Gallup poll findings covering the years 1939–60 indicate that union families voted 6·7% more pro-Democrat than the average for all manual-worker families, union members 12% more pro-Democrat than non-union workers. They show that these differentials are widest when and where unions are most active politically: the pro-Democrat differential between unionist and non-unionist workers for example, went up to 20% during the Presidential campaign of 1956.

What is this help worth to the Democrats? One academic analyst estimates their net basic gain from organized labour's intervention at less than one million votes: other estimates range up to three million. In the elections of 1952 and 1956 the pro-Democratic ballots cast by unionists in two industrialized states, New Jersey and Illinois, amounted to only one-third of the total union membership figure in each – turnouts distinctly below the national average proportion of all non-unionist Americans in those years. But the point is not how many votes

11

absolutely, but how distributed. Union leaders have never seriously claimed they could deliver large blocs, only that they could crucially affect the size of the urban majorities. There is evidence that from 1960 onwards COPE has been concentrating its precinct activity upon marginal constituencies where critical shifts to Democratic candidates can be achieved. In 1968 it was broadly true that the larger the city, above half-a-million populace, the bigger the Humphrey vote.

Let us try to sum up the present situation. For one reason and another, labour in American politics remains a minority group of qualified popularity, and its leaders are well aware of the fact. It cannot buck the political tide in any election, but in close and uncertain races it can provide the margin of victory. To retain this degree of political significance it must for the foreseeable future preserve its special relationship with the Democratic party. As a pressure group it must seek coalitions, and the most congenial allies are usually to be found among small liberal groups outside the purely industrial arena. These circumstances oblige union leaders in the political sphere to commit themselves to a vastly wider concept of the obligations of unionism than in the merely economic. In so doing they and their followers can constitute by far the largest and most stable body supporting liberal causes in the United States today. If this assessment is of potential rather than performance, it is not the less just for that.

Appendix: Further reading

General

The most considerable general *History of Labor in the United States* up to 1932 is the four-volume work of that title by John R. Commons and his associates. Among recent single-volume studies are Philip Taft's detailed *Organized Labor in American History* (1964) and the more general surveys by Joseph G. Rayback: *A History of American Labor* (2nd ed., 1966) and Henry M. Pelling: *American Labor* (1960).

A fair selection of relevant documents has been edited by Charles H. Rehmus and D. B. McLaughlin under the title *Labor and American Politics* (1967).

Texts of important statutes affecting labour and excerpts from the more important Supreme Court cases, with commentary, are to be found in Russell A. Smith & L. S. Merrifield: *Cases and Materials on Labor Relations Law* (revised edit. plus supplements, 1960–) and in Jerre S. Williams: *Labor Relations and the Law* (3rd ed., 1965). Selected cases are wrapped in discussion in Harry H. Wellington: *Labor and the Legal Process* (1968).

1 Labour and the American environment

Labour's political enterprises before the New Deal are variously treated by Nathan Fine: *Labor and Farmer Parties in the United States, 1828–1928* (1961), by Norman J. Ware: *The Labour Movement in the United States, 1860–1895* (1929) and by Gerald N. Grob: *Workers and Utopia, 1865–1900* (1960).

The violence of the American experience is emphasized in Samuel

Yellen: *American Labor Struggles* (1956) and Louis Adamic: *Dynamite* (1931). Henry David has interpreted *The History of the Haymarket Affair* (1936), Wayne J. Broehl *The Molly Maguires* (1964), Almont Lindsey *The Pullman Strike* (1942), and Leon Wolff the Homestead strike in *Lockout* (1965).

Among autobiographies of labour leaders should be noted Terence Powderley's *The Path I Trod* (1940), and among biographies Ray Ginger's of Debs, *The Bending Cross* (1949) and Murray B. Seidler's *Norman Thomas, Respectable Rebel* (1961). Kenneth C. MacKay's *The Progressive Movement of 1924* (1947) gives La Follette his due.

Howard H. Quint has chronicled *The Forging of American Socialism* (1953), and the story is taken further by Ira Kipnis: *The American Socialist Movement, 1897–1912* (1952) and David Shannon: *The Socialist Party of America* (1955). The IWW is best understood through Patrick Renshaw: *The Wobblies* (1967) and communism through the account of a practitioner, William Z. Foster: *History of the Communist Party of the United States* (1952). A British socialist, Harold J. Laski, voiced his discontent with American union political activity in his *Trade Unions and the New Society* (1950).

2 The voluntarism of Samuel Gompers

Gompers's own writings include his two-volume autobiography, *Seventy Years of Life and Labor* (1948), *Labor in Europe and America* (1910), *Labor and the Common Welfare* (1919), and a compilation of his public utterances by Hayes Robbins: *Labor and the Employer* (1920). The best biography is B. Mandel: *Samuel Gompers* (1963).

The most comprehensive study of the field is Philip Taft: *The A.F. of L. in the Time of Gompers* (1957), which does not however efface Lewis L. Lorwin's pre-New Deal *The American Federation of Labor* (1933). Labour's legal handicaps throughout this period are examined severally in F. Frankfurter & N. Greene: *The Labor Injunction* (1930), Joel Seidman: *Yellow-Dog Contract* (1932), Edward Berman: *Labor and the Sherman Act* (1930), and (for the Clayton Act) Charles O. Gregory: *Labor and the Law* (1949); and generally in Alpheus T. Mason: *Organized Labor and the Law* (1925) and Edwin E. Witte: *Government in Labor Disputes* (1932).

Valuable episodic studies are Marguerite Green: *The National Civic Federation and the American Labor Movement* (1956), Gordon S. Watkins: *Labor Problems and Labor Administration during the World War* (1919), Marc Carson: *American Labor in Politics, 1900–1918* (1958) and James O. Morris: *Conflict Within the American*

Federation of Labor, 1901–1938 (1958). The many accounts of the depression include Broadus Mitchell: *Depression Decade* (1947) and Dixon Wecter: *The Age of the Great Depression* (1948).

3 The new government of Franklin Roosevelt

The vast literature of the New Deal makes selection even more than usually arbitrary. Labour's interests emerge *passim* from Arthur M. Schlesinger, Jr's, *The Age of Roosevelt* (1957–); and Milton Derber and Edwin Young have edited a very useful volume of essays, *Labor and the New Deal* (1957). Roosevelt's own economic philosophy is explored in Daniel R. Fusfeld: *The Economic Thought of Franklin D. Roosevelt* (1956).

Relevant facets of his government's policy are studied by Lewis Meriam: *Relief and Social Security* (1946), Orme W. Phelps: *The Legislative Background of the Fair Labor Standards Act* (1939); and for the Wagner Act in particular, Joseph Rosenfarb: *National Labor Policy and How it Works* (1940) and Irving Bernstein: *New Deal Collective Bargaining Policy* (1950). The unions' need of legal protection and encouragement, as revealed by the La Follette committee, is the theme of Jerold S. Auerbach: *Labor and Liberty* (1966). The new policies are seen through the eyes of the Secretary of Labour in Frances Perkins: *The Roosevelt I Knew* (1946) and through those of the old-style labour leader in Matthew Woll: *Labor, Industry and Government* (1935) and Saul D. Alinsky: *John L. Lewis* (1949). A socialist critique of the New Deal is contained in the pamphlets of Norman Thomas, particularly his *The New Deal, a social analysis* (1933) and *After the New Deal – What?* (1936).

The split in the labour movement is recorded by Herbert Harris: *Labor's Civil War* (1940) and by Walter Galenson: *The CIO Challenge to the AFL* (1960); the new organizing drives by Edwin Levinson: *Labor on the March* (1938) and Benjamin Stolberg: *The Story of the CIO* (1938).

4 The new model of Sidney Hillman

The most thorough study of labour in World War II is Joel Seidman's *American Labor from Defense to Reconversion* (1953). Items of Presidential policy are reprinted in Samuel I. Rosenman (ed.): *The Public Papers and Addresses of F. D. Roosevelt*, vols. 9 to 13 (1940–5). The roles played by Hillman himself during these years, as well as a minute account of his life, are described in Matthew Josephson: *Sidney Hillman, Statesman of American Labor* (1952).

This last work also describes the genesis and early activity of the CIO-PAC, items of whose 1944 propaganda have been collected with a commentary by Joseph Gaer: *The First Round* (1944). More detailed information on this subject can be gleaned – though copies are scarce in Britain – from the *Hearings* and *Reports* of special committees examining campaign expenditures in House and Senate of the 78th. and 79th. Congresses (1944–5) as listed in the publications catalogues of the Government Printing Office, Washington, D.C.

Two contrasting books reveal the contemporary disquiet at the enhanced power of organized labour – Thurman Arnold's *Bottlenecks of Business* (1940) and Louis G. Silverberg's *The Wagner Act after Ten Years* (1945). Lewis's conduct during the war is noted by Saul D. Alinsky (in the work already listed for Chapter 3 above) and by James A. Wechsler: *Labor Baron* (1944).

Much of labour's planning literature for the post-war world was ephemeral: but how one goal was fulfilled by the Murray Employment Act is described in Stephen K. Bailey: *Congress Makes a Law* (1950). An interesting post-war conspectus is Sidney Lens: *Left, Right and Center in American Labor* (1949); and C. Wright Mills: *The New Men of Power* (1948) is a highly personal evaluation.

5 The conservatism of Senator Taft

For the American Federation of Labour the story is carried on by Philip Taft in *The A.F. of L. from the Death of Gompers to the Merger* (1959), which contains material relevant to Chapters 3 and 4 also. There is an account of the merger itself by the CIO's former General Counsel, Arthur J. Goldberg, in his *AFL-CIO, Labor United* (1956).

The course of legislative control over collective bargaining is followed by H. A. Mills & E. C. Brown: *From the Wagner Act to Taft-Hartley* (1950): the situation on the morrow of Taft-Hartley is surveyed by Glen W. Miller: *American Labor and the Government* (1948), and the state of affairs by 1960 is set out succinctly in the International Labour Office's report of that year, *The Trade Union Situation in the United States*, and at greater length by D. F. MacDonald: *The State and the Trade Unions* (1960). Among much literary protest by the unions over Taft-Hartley may be mentioned the CIO's *The Case Against Right-to-Work Laws* (1954).

Communism in trade unions is the subject of Max M. Kampelman's *The Communist Party and the CIO* (1957) and a significant part of G. A. Werner's *American Communism* (1947). Racketeering is one theme of Sidney Lens: *The Crisis of American Labor* (1959), to which Robert D. Leiter's study of *The Teamsters Union* (1957) is also pertinent. Passage through Congress of the so-called Landrum-Griffin Act is traced in detail by Alan K. McAdams: *Power and Politics in Labor Legislation* (1964), and through the House in particular in Chapter 8 of Richard Bollings: *House Out of Order* (1965).

For minorities, Ray Marshall looks at *The Negro and Organized Labor* (1966), while a number of court decisions involving minority rights of trade unionists are recorded in T. I. Emerson, D. Haber & N. Dorsen: *Political and Civil Rights in the United States* (2 vols., student edit., 1967).

Predictions for labour's future are mixed in William Haber (ed.): *Labor in a Changing America* and rather gloomy in Solomon Barkin's pamphlet *The Decline of the Labor Movement* (1961). But the rise of a forward-looking union leader is chronicled in I. Howe & R. J. Riddick: *The UAW and Walter Reuther* (1949) and his social faith expounded in his *Selected Papers* (ed. Henry M. Christman, 1961).

6 Modes of engagement

There is no single extended study of unions as a pressure group, but a number of scattered articles and papers refer to it. Some of these are collected in (e.g.) the *Proceedings* of the American Academy of Political and Social Sciences, vols. 274 (March 1951) and 319 (September 1958), and in such compilations as H. R. Mahood (ed.): *Pressure Groups in American Politics* (1967). The variety of labour's relationships with state party organizations is well illustrated by Fay Calkins: *The CIO and the Democratic Party* (1952).

Early labour lobbying is noted *obiter* in Lorwin's book on *The American Federation of Labor* already cited for Chapter 2, and in Harwood L. Childs: *Labor and Capital in National Politics* (1930). The forms of present-day labour lobbying may be discerned in the studies by McAdams and Bolling recommended for the preceding chapter. The growing representation of labour in the federal administration up to World War II is traced in J. Lombardi: *Labor's Voice in the Cabinet* (1942).

Something of the extent of union political activity can be learnt from the national and state convention *Proceedings* of AFL, CIO and AFL-CIO, nowadays published biennially, but possibly more from testimony given to Congressional committees such as the House select committee of Lobbying activities during the 81st. Congress (1950), the House special committee on Campaign Expenditures of the 82nd. (1952) and the Senate sub-committee on Privileges and Elections of the 84th. (1956). The financial implication of such engagement is considered by Alexander Heard as part of *The Costs of*

Democracy (1960) and by V. Vale: 'American Labour's Political Freedom', in *Political Studies*, vol. 13, No. 3 (October 1965). The *Congressional Quarterly* publishes regular digests of campaign and lobbying expenditures by trade unions.

The impact of unions' political propaganda on their membership is assessed in a number of studies, notably by A. Kornhauser *et al.*: *When Labor Votes* (1956), H. and R. A. H. Rosen: *The Union Member Speaks* (1955), and here and there in Angus Campbell *et al.*: *The Voter Decides* (1954) and *The American Voter* (1960).

Index